The

Wigwam

Murder

The
Wigwam
Murder

M.J. Trow

This second edition published 2016 worldwide by
T Squared Books.
www.tsquaredbooks.co.uk

Copyright © 2016 M. J. Trow

First published in 1994 by Constable.

A CIP catalogue record for this book is available from the British
Library.

ISBN: 978-0-9954521-4-5

T SQUARED BOOKS

To Mam

With thanks for her reminiscences of the war

(and for teaching me to write!)

Acknowledgements

My thanks to all who have contributed to this book.

To those who lived in the Thursley area in 1942 – ex-PC A.W. Bundy, Miss P.J. Dummer, Mr A.E. Gale.

To those who knew Joan Wolfe – Mrs R. Durrant, Mrs Betty Holliday and others.

To 'the Canadians' – Carl Goddard, Carol White of the Personnel Records Centre, National Archives of Canada and Mrs Helen McKay of the Battleford Branch Library.

To Linda Findlay of the Surrey Police Headquarters Press Office.

To Michael Page of the Archivist's Department, Surrey County Council.

To Joan Charman, Librarian of the Goldalming Trust.

To G.R. Collyer, Editor of the *Surrey Advertiser*.

To Mrs Carolyn Smith, Educational Psychologist of the Isle of Wight County Council.

To all authors and publishers from whose works I have quoted.

To my wife, Carol, for all her hours of labour at the keyboard and her continued help and support.

Contents

Acknowledgements

Foreword

Chapter 1 – The Girl in the Wood

Chapter 2 – There Was a War On

Chapter 3 – Joan Pearl Wolfe

Chapter 4 – The Lovers

Chapter 5 – Softly, Softly …

Chapter 6 – 'Fit to Stand His Trial'

Chapter 7 – Métis

Chapter 8 – Who Killed the Wigwam Girl

Afterword

Bibliography

Foreword

I wrote *Let Him Have It, Chris*, on the Craig and Bentley case, in 1990, not only because it was a clear and notorious miscarriage of justice, but because I realised that educationally limited people like Derek Bentley, hanged for a crime he did not commit in 1953, stood little chance against the behemoth of the British criminal justice system.

It occurred to me, as a teacher used to dealing with the educationally challenged, that there must be other cases where an accused was effectively railroaded by the iniquities of the law. One was Engin Raghip, accused of the horrific murder of PC Keith Blakelock in the Broadwater Farm riots in October 1985. The man was said, in various Press reports, to be educationally sub-normal (in the phraseology of the time) and I wondered how he would even start to cope with the high-fallutin' language of the court. When the prosecution against Raghip failed, a second 'culprit', Winston Silcott, appeared in the dock, charged with Blakelock's murder. On appeal, this too fell apart and today, Keith Blakelock has had no justice at all, his family waiting in what must be a limbo of despair.

The third example I came across was August Sangret, a Canadian Métis with a lamentable lack of education, who was hanged in 1943 for the murder of his girlfriend, Joan Wolfe. Since the Blakelock case was still open, I concentrated on this case, known as the Wigwam Murder and quickly realised that Sangret did not fit the bill. His schooling was almost non-existent and, like Derek Bentley, he was functionally illiterate. That said, he was vocal, involved, of average intelligence (as opposed to Bentley's IQ of 66) and eminently 'fit to stand his trial'. By that time, however, I was hooked on the star-crossed lovers whose affair ended in bloody tragedy in a Surrey woodland in the middle of a world war and I finished the book anyway.

What you will read here is the transcript as it was written in 1994, with few editorial changes. John Major was Prime Minister and the political problems that dominate today – Islamic fundamentalism and the leaving of the European Union – scarcely registered in news reports. Women priests were ordained for the first time and the police were tied up with an altogether more macabre murder scene, the house of Fred and Rose West, Gloucester's own serial killers. The book was published by Constable & Co, then still an independent with offices in Fulham Palace Road, London.

M J Trow
June 2016

1

The Girl in the Wood

Hankley Common, now. The Grey Goose Moon. A knife's throw from the busy A31 and the busier A3, where traffic races north-east to bypass the bottleneck that is Guildford and to join the nightmare that is the M25. Large, opulent houses are set back from the road, ringed with neat lawns and rhododendron bushes and studded with burglar alarms; middle-class, Home Counties Britain in the days of recession.

Drive south-west from Milford Crossroads; go back, back in time. Look at the older maps; the older names. Hammer Pond, the Moat, Houndown, Pitlands, the Devil's Jumps. Take the minor roads, twisting through the countryside as they did before the Highway Code. Leave the car under the pines and climb to the heights of Kettlebury Hill. Here it is exposed, lonely. The only sound is the moan of the wind in the wires. On all sides stretch sandy dunes and yellow coarse clumps of grass. The mixed forest of conifers lies, a darker green, among the deciduous birches; the heather, carpets of purple and mauve, makes spring pathways.

The trees have grown up. Seventy years on, they clothe the slopes of Houndown Wood. Count the rings of those that have been felled; they would have been saplings then. Duck under the conifers that the hurricane of 1987 brought down across the dell. Here the bracken is thick, the leaves are a brown carpet of decay. Stand still. Listen. It was here. Here the deadly dance began.

She ran this way; forwards, down towards the stream, towards the road. It wasn't far – two or three hundred yards. Here, where the tripwire lay, are her teeth still buried, smashed from her gums. She didn't make it, in the still early morning, as his stronger legs closed the distance between then and the blood filled her eyes and dripped from her ripped arms. The birches still stare down from the hill, silent witnesses.

The chase ended at the stream, at the slit-trench in the mossy hollow where her head was smashed to a pulp, where her skull disintegrated and her breath stopped. He rolled her sideways under the leaves. He saw her face, a mask of blood, her front teeth gone, her right cheek shattered, the dark stain spreading over her thin, green cotton dress. He left her under the blanket. He had to be elsewhere, before they missed him.

On that hilltop, now covered with conifers, he dragged her – what? Two, three days later? – in the darkness of a September night. She was still lying in the leaf mould. The last flies of summer droned upwards at his approach. Did he look at her face under the stars? The red blood turned brown and caked hard? The laughing eyes now cold and dull and still. By the left arm he dragged her, face down now, her bare legs ripped by brambles. Not long before, they'd picked those blackberries together and laughed and tickled each other, as lovers will. Children had watched them, curious in the upside down world they lived in; nosiness that would be honed to a razor in the confines of a court of law. Her shoes fell off as her dead feet bounced on the bracken, 16 yards to the first shoe, 35 to the second. Then up the steep bracken-deep hill to the top, to the high ground, where the tanks trained. To the sky.

The army is still here. Signs read 'Troops training – there may be sudden movements and noises near paths and bridleways.' There are black Nissen huts, khaki vehicles, perimeter fences. After seventy years, the army is still here.

On Hankley Common, then – Wednesday, 7 October 1942 – the Moon the Birds Fly South – among the picturesque moorland of the Surrey-Sussex border 'with its gentle hills topped with bracken and heather, fir trees and silver birch', between Godalming and the Hog's Back, more than 100,000 American and Canadian troops were camped. One woman who walked here in those days was Molly Lefebure, who remembered the area in *Evidence for the Crown*:

> 'Hankley Common was a former beauty spot, all heathery slopes, broken with graceful spinneys of birch and oak and surrounded by wide vistas of wooded countryside and windswept sky. The Army, noting its loveliness, had of course taken it over as a battle-training ground. Camps had been built in the neighbouring woods and every day young men were taken out and toughened up amid a welter of anti-tank obstacles, mortar ranges, field telephones and trip-wires.'

Chief Inspector Edward Greeno of Scotland Yard knew it too:

> '… the whole panorama of the plain, pitted with tank traps and pimpled with those man-made mounds.'

There was a war on and on that day the Marines were exercising in the sand dunes. POX 100381 William Moore RM was patrolling the area on a routine march. Everywhere the ground was rutted by the iron teeth of tanks, lurching over the heather in search of phoney enemies with blackened faces and leaves wound round their helmets. In one such tank track, at a little before 10.20 Ack Emma, Moore saw what appeared to be a human hand protruding from a mound of earth. He crouched beside it. The thumb and the first two fingers had been gnawed away, as though by rats. There was a foot too, protruding at the other end of what was clearly a human body. Moore did not touch the grisly find, but reported it at once to Sergeant CHX 103272 Jack Withington RM, who, in the tradition of all services, passed the information on up the line, this time to Lieutenant Norman McLeod. The officer joined his men on the hillside and took one look. Then he telephoned the police.

It was Sergeant Benjamin Ballard of the Surrey constabulary stationed at Milford who arrived at the scene, together with Constable AW Bundy from Thursley. In the emergency situation of wartime, police forces throughout the country, especially those on the fringes of London, had to take extraordinary measures to cope with the extraordinary demands made on them. The Surrey force was now a joint one, along with the police of the boroughs of Reigate and Guildford. With hindsight at the trial which followed, Ballard was able to testify that the hand in the mound belonged to a woman, but there was nothing on that Wednesday to verify this. Even the protruding foot at the opposite end of the mound gave little away, except that the body seemed to be lying face down in a shallow and makeshift grave.

By evening the full panoply of the law was in action and a knot of trilby-hatted, trench-coated policemen stood grim-faced inside a cordon around which uniformed officers patrolled, still in their upright Victorian collars, their gas masks and tin hats in canvas bags at their hips. Superintendent Richard Webb, stationed at Godalming, had been informed at 4 pm. He ordered the mound to be covered with a mackintosh sheet. He noted that the earth was criss-crossed with the tyre tracks of a military vehicle, probably a half-track, and it was this which had displaced the earth sufficiently to reveal the hand and leg. Strange how incidents like this interfere with cunning. The best laid plans of mice and men . . .

Twenty-four hours later, Webb was accompanied by Major Nicholson, the Chief Constable of Surrey, Superintendent Thomas Roberts, head of the Surrey CID, and police photographer Inspector Eric Boshier as they made their way to the murder scene. With them was Dr Eric Gardner, consulting pathologist at Weybridge Hospital, and Dr Keith Simpson, lecturer in forensic medicine at Guy's Hospital. With them too was Molly Lefebure, Simpson's secretary.

> 'Greetings were exchanged and then off we set to climb a windy ridge which reared itself, rain-swept and dismal, ahead of us. It is odd how it invariably begins to rain when one reaches the scene of a crime …'

Miss Lefebure, young, inexperienced, female, remembers shivering in the cold, trying to warm herself by smoking.

> 'Few young journalists [wrote Simpson years later] can have had the remarkable experience that befell Molly Lefebure on her translation from 'crime and news' reporter on a London newspaper to a job then quite unique – private secretary to a pathologist engaged in scientific crime detection in and around the metropolis of London.'

Molly Lefebure had studied journalism at London University and in 1939-40 was working as a reporter on a chain of East London weeklies. She walked, she later wrote, on average twelve miles a day, working from eight thirty in the morning until ten thirty at night, seven days a week. Her take-home pay was £1. She covered everything from Boy Scout meetings to the Blitz. But something within her drew her to the coroner's court and police court like a moth to a flame. It was here that she met Simpson:

> 'He certainly looked remarkable; there was something of genius about him, a hint of lightning flashes and thunderbolts. I frequently mused upon his unique but intriguing occupation, wondering whether cutting up

bodies all day long had any effect upon the cutter-upper ...'

Cedric Keith Simpson – CKS to colleagues and friends – was thirty-five at the time. His rise had been meteoric. The son of a doctor from Brighton, he had been educated at Brighton and Hove Grammar School and entered Guy's Hospital Medical School in 1924. Here, he won all the glittering prizes – the Hilton prize for dissection, the Wooldridge prize for physiology, the Beaney prize for pathology, the Golding-Bird gold medal and a scholarship in bacteriology. After he qualified in 1930 he joined the clinical staff at Guy's and became a lecturer in pathology there in 1932. Five years later he began to devote himself entirely to forensic medicine – hence his constant appearance in the courts which Molly Lefebure frequented.

It was the heyday of the forensic scientist. Donald Teare and Francis Camps were his contemporaries and Simpson often crossed swords with them in court. Over them all however was the almost legendary figure of the gaunt, hollow-eyed Bernard Spilsbury. 'These were the days,' Simpson wrote with hindsight in 1954, 'when Spilsbury was fading.' The honorary Pathologist to the Home Office killed himself shortly before Christmas 1947.

On that damp Surrey hillside, Simpson, assured, steady, every inch the professional, only remembers taking off his jacket in the heat. 'The stench of putrefaction was strong,' he wrote in *Forty Years of Murder*, 'the air was buzzing with flies and the remains of the body were crawling with maggots.' He estimated that it must have lain exposed to the air for long enough for blowflies to have settled and laid their eggs. There were, he told the police, two or three successive egg-layings. The body would have been partially covered first, perhaps with leaves or a blanket.

Tom Roberts remembered the scene years later in his autobiography, *Friends and Villains*.

'… the grave was shallow and the soil light and sandy. Decomposition was well advanced, the skull had collapsed and most of the soft tissue of the head and neck and lower parts of the body had been completely eaten away by maggots.'

Together, Simpson and Gardner, who were old friends and had worked on cases as team before, began to scrape away the earth with shovels. Everyone who could moved out of the wind to escape the stench, but the stoical Miss Lefebure stood by CKS taking from the pathologists specimens of beetles, maggots, earth and heather, carefully labelling them in separate buff envelopes. The police photographer angled his shots and the camera popped and flashed on that rainy hillside.

The body was clearly that of a woman, lying face down in the Surrey soil, the remnants of her clothing clinging to her decomposing form, her legs apart, her left arm stretched forward as though she had been dragged. Her hand and leg were becoming mummified and parts of her had been eaten by rats. The head in particular was on the point of disintegration, a seething mass of maggots. She was wearing a tatty green and white summer frock with a lace collar, fastened around the waist with string. Her underclothing consisted of a slip, vest, brassiere and French knickers, all of it shabby. A headscarf was tied loosely around her neck and she wore short ankle socks but no shoes.

Kneeling by her side, Simpson speculated on the cause of death: 'A heavy blunt instrument, perhaps an iron bar or a wooden pole or stake.' In his mind were wilder speculations which it was not his business to voice: 'A sex assault and strangling? Concealment after a stabbing in London or an abortion death in some nearby city?' And most prophetically) although cheating, I suspect, with hindsight): 'A ritual burial on a hilltop.'

Dr Gardner estimated, from the extent of the flowering heather around the body, that the woman had been buried five or six weeks earlier. Gardner, the local man, knew his heaths. The heather finished flowering about the beginning of September. That took the likely time of the murder to the end of August or early September, the Snow Goose Moon; an important initial 'timing' for the police, but one that was to be proved wrong by between two and three weeks.

It was clearly impossible to learn more from the rotting corpse *in situ* so Gardner and Simpson contacted the coroner, Dr Wills Taylor, who gave permission for it to be taken to Guy's for the week's work in the laboratory that Simpson estimated would be necessary. They wrapped what was left of her in a waterproof sheet.

> 'Maggots seethed out of the chest and abdominal cavity [Simpson wrote later] and by tea-time thousands more were struggling for life in a carbolic bath in Guy's Hospital Mortuary.'

Molly Lefebure was heartily glad that she had not had to travel back to London in the police van with the corpse.

Cases like that of the body on the common formed only part of Keith Simpson's work. As Home Office Pathologist, he has rightly won a place as one of the greatest of forensic scientists, dominating the middle years of the century.

Guy's Hospital, where the body now lay, was founded in 1721 by Thomas Guy, bookseller and printer, who made a fortune in speculation and endowed a number of charitable foundations. The original block, Guy's House, built in 1729, had been badly damaged by bombs in 1941 when Simpson was working there as Assistant Curator in the Gordon Museum. Three months before the body at Hankley Common was found, the great man had led his assistant, S F Ireland, and Molly Lefebure into a tiny room off the Department of Clinical Chemistry. 'Miss Lefebure, Ireland,' he announced with a flourish, 'allow me to usher you across the threshold of Guy's Hospital Department of Forensic Medicine.' Ireland was carrying a microscope, Molly Lefebure a typewriter and

Simpson the remains of what turned out to be Mrs Dobkin, murdered by her husband Harry in another spectacular case which effectively launched the department. As such, it is worthy of discussion.

There was a war on. And one of the targets of that war, whether wittingly or not, was a Baptist Chapel in the Vauxhall Road, Lambeth. Workmen hacking with pick and shovel to clear the debris found a partially mummified corpse under the shattered flagstones. It was 17 July 1942, a date we shall meet again. The remains were taken to Southwark Mortuary where Simpson went to work. The body was that of a woman (her mummified womb was still in place) and she was not a victim of the bomb blast. In fact, she had been quite carefully buried in slaked lime and its yellow deposits still clung to the corpse.

Simpson reassembled the bones, and the macabre jigsaw, using Pearson's formulae (then the most reliable technique for gauging height) produced the result that the dead woman was 5ft ½in tall. She was between forty and fifty and her hair was dark brown, turning grey. Beyond that, all recognizable features had disappeared. A swelling in the uterus and the survival of the teeth in the dead woman's upper jaw proved beyond a shadow of a doubt however that she was Rachel Dobkin, aged forty-seven, the estranged wife of the local fire-watcher, who had vanished fifteen months earlier on her way to visit her husband over a matter of arrears of maintenance.

'That's my patient!' [Mrs Dobkin's dentist] burst out excitedly on seeing her skull upturned on Simpson's bench at Guy's. 'That's Mrs Dobkin! Those are my fillings!'

> 'It was as dramatic a moment as I can remember [Simpson wrote]. Molly Lefebure nearly fell off her lab stool.'

The jury took twenty minutes to find Harry Dobkin guilty of murdering his wife at the Old Bailey in November. He was hanged at Wandsworth Prison, on 27 January 1943.

The 'department' at Guy's measured 10 feet by 5 and when all three of its members were there, accompanied frequently by portions of a corpse, it appeared very small indeed. A bench ran the length of one wall and above it a single window gave a view of a brick wall and the smoky Southwark sky. There were two stools, a number of reference books, a set of weighing scales and a huge blotter. The whole room had been lent to Simpson by Dr Ryffel, Head of Clinical Chemistry. It was his weighing room.

By 1942, the worst of the blitz was over but London was still a city in turmoil. Everywhere were the craters of incendiary bombs and the shells of buildings. Simpson's work was an endless round of post-mortems, police courts, coroners' courts, magistrates' courts, the Old Bailey. With Molly Lefebure in tow, he visited prisons, hospitals, asylums – 'the alleys and filthy courtyards and tenements of Limehouse, Rotherhithe, Poplar, Shoreditch, Bethnal Green, Whitechapel, Stratford-by-Bow' – the decayed wreck of the still-Victorian Metropolis. Then there were the 'amazing no-man's-land of the suburbs' and 'the West End . . . plushy, well-washed, but with its sordid secrets in Chelsea, Westminster, Marylebone.'

It was the day of the spiv and the black marketeer. And a young airman named Gordon Cummins had left a trail of terror in London with four corpses mutilated in the space of five days. With all this going on and the Metropolitan Police stretched to breaking point, Simpson examined the Hankley Common corpse in his tea-breaks, much to Miss Lefebure's disgust, alongside the carbolic tank in which the body floated. They sat with their teacakes and anchovy toast while Simpson worked on the cadaver, occasionally assisted by Gardner, who came up from Surrey for the purpose. By this means, Simpson was able to answer all the questions the police would need to ask in order to ascertain who this woman was and how she had died.

He at first agreed with Gardner that she had died between five and seven weeks before she'd been found. He later revised this to a month, based on the extent of adipocere in the breasts and thighs. This is a whitish, fatty substance which occurs in damp conditions. It smells and feels horrible and clings to the bone, retaining the body's usual shape. The process – known as saponification – by which neutral body fats are hydrolysed into a mixture of fatty acids and soap, normally takes five to six weeks to reach the stage it had in this case, but Simpson realized that the huge presence of maggots would have generated heat, accelerating the process considerably. So the woman had probably died in the middle of September.

He then turned his attention to the cause of death. The dead woman's skull had been shattered by a single, very violent blow. The head had all but collapsed and Simpson and Gardner spent three days carefully piecing and wiring together the thirty-eight major pieces of the skull. At the back was a gaping hole, 1¾ inches across, which was the site of the impact. The length of the entire impact area was 5¼ inches. From this at least six fractures radiated outwards, three, which Simpson was to number 4, 5 and 6, to the base of the skull, and three (1, 2 and 3) across the top, number 2 following a suture line. The pieces of bone left in a pile on Simpson's bench belonged to the gaping hole, but there were lots of them, each one too small to reconstruct. A second area of the same width and contiguous with the hole indicated that a heavy blunt instrument with a diameter of 1¾ inches and of indeterminate length had been brought down diagonally across the back of the head. It followed then that her killer had struck from behind. The blow would have caused loss of consciousness immediately and death within a few minutes, from shock and brain damage.

It was not as simple as that, however. There was a series of stab wounds at the front of the skull and on top, but without any skin or flesh remaining, Simpson was unable to tell whether these had been delivered before or after death. There were three holes, grouped close together on the top left of the head, indicating that whoever made them had attacked with his right hand while facing his victim. Simpson checked the right arm, the one that would naturally be raised to ward off such an attack. Although Simpson maintains this in *Forty Years of Murder* and was to offer it in hypothesis at the trial, the notion seems flawed. It is the *left* arm of the victim which is nearer to a right-handed attacker striking from the front. A right-handed person would probably raise both arms in defence. Similar stab wounds peppered this arm and microscopic evidence proved that these where inflicted while the victim was still very much alive, fighting in fact for her life.

In *Murder What Dunnit*, J.H.H. Gauté and Robin Odell say that the knife 'superseded the axe and the bludgeon, lending subtlety and concealment to the act of killing'. This was clearly not so here, as both blade and bludgeon were used – and subtlety is hardly the word for the fatal blow in this case.

Knife attacks constitute two types – the cut, incision or slash as exemplified in the Ripper murders of 1888 and the stab, as here. The latter produces small slits at the point of entry which often cause relatively little bleeding. As these wounds were to the head, however, Simpson assumed that bleeding was profuse. A single-edged weapon would leave a 'tear-drop' shape, as opposed to the shallow ellipse of a double-edged knife. In this case, however, there was no flesh left on the head and the wounds on the skull were virtually circular, looking for all the world like counter-sunk screw holes. Chief Inspector Greeno likened them to the work of a brace and bit.

From this, Simpson was able to establish the likely course of events. Two of the three holes in the front of the head were shallow cuts. They were probably delivered first, would have caused great pain, dizziness and possibly later collapse, but the woman would still have been able to run away. The front teeth were missing from the upper jaw and this could have been caused by a fall or by a fist to the mouth. The fracture to the victim's right cheek, however, cleared this dilemma up. It was a crush fracture which had separated the cheekbone and was commensurate with the fatal blow to the back of the skull having been struck while she lay face down on the ground. One of the radiating cracks in the skull had virtually reached this bone below the right eye socket.

The murder weapon, Simpson had already decided, was likely to be a pole or bough – and in Houndown Wood, a mixture of coniferous and deciduous woodland, such things were hardly in short supply. The knife that caused the stab wounds, however, was highly distinctive and it led with deadly accuracy to the man apparently guilty of murder. The wound in the right forearm and another on the palm of the right hand had the curious feature of tissue and tendons pulled out of the slit, as though by a sharp hook. The wounds to the front of the skull had bevelled edges, as though the point of the weapon had been twisted before withdrawal. Why should the murderer have done that? To inflict greater pain? Or because a peculiarity in the knife gave him no choice if he was to retrieve it to strike again? Simpson was therefore able to tell the police that they were looking for a knife with a blade like a parrot's beak.

The victim's brain had gone. Her face had gone. But she told an eloquent story still.

On two points she remained silent. Dr Eric Gardner at the trial which followed was asked whether he and Simpson had examined the woman to see if she had been pregnant. His reply was that it always occurred to pathologists to do this in the case of young female corpses, but that not enough of the uterus remained to be positive on this point. Something of the shame of an unwanted pregnancy still lingered in Britain in 1942, for all there was a war on. There were scores of women living in wretched conditions in mental hospitals and asylums because they had 'fallen' (note the vituperative word) pregnant in their teens. It was still a motive for murder. Simpson agreed that the generations of gases after death might well have dissolved the foetus anyway. The other imponderable – and one that had to be cleared up quickly for any headway to be made at all – was: who was the dead girl?

Simpson was able to provide a working description of the girl, although her face was beyond recognition. The X-rays of her bones and the state of her teeth indicated that she was between nineteen and twenty. She was 5 feet 4 inches tall with a small frame. Her hair was fine, a mousy-brown colour, probably worn in the then fashionable bobbed style, and had been bleached some weeks earlier. The most distinctive feature about her, oddly enough, could be gauged by the angle of her missing front teeth – they had protruded significantly.

The clothing was unhelpful, but the fact that she was wearing brassier, slip and knickers indicated that sexual assault was not involved. It was the green and white summer frock, however that rang bells with Superintendent Webb of the Surrey force who visited Guy's on the day that Simpson removed the clothing. He had seen that frock briefly in his own office on 23 July and again in August for rather longer. At her own instigation, the girl wearing it had gone to a local hospital. Her name was Joan Pearl Wolfe. She was nineteen and had had protruding teeth. There was no need for the elaborate reconstruction of the dead girl's face which Professor Brash had created in the Ruxton case some years earlier.

At the end of September 1935, a woman crossing Gardenholme Linn, a tributary of the River Annan, on the road between Carlisle and Edinburgh, saw a human arm lying in the mud below her. Subsequent police investigation revealed the dismembered remains of two female bodies, wrapped, like old chips, in the *Sunday Graphic* for 15 September. This particular edition was sold only in the Morecambe and Lancaster areas and eventually the two women were traced to Bukhtyar Ratanji Hakim, a Parsee doctor living in Lancaster and practising under the mercifully simpler Anglicized name of Buck Ruxton. His common law wife, Isabella Van Ess, had left him, he said, for another man. And her maid, Mary Rogerson, had taken the opportunity to leave too.

Forensically, the two corpses in the river mud matched in general terms, but the specifics were less neat. Mary Rogerson had an obvious squint, but the eyes had been removed. Isabella 'Ruxton', like Joan Wolfe, had prominent front teeth. These, too, had gone. She also had a deformed left foot and this was mutilated.

Professors Glaister and Brash, working out of Edinburgh University, pieced together the seventy pieces which the two women had been extended to. Brash's superimposed photograph of Isabella 'Ruxton' over the skull of one body has become legendary and features in most modern forensic books.

Ruxton, who admitted screaming rows with his wife, had tried to hawk a woman's bloodstained suit recently and carpets at his home were found to be bloodstained too. He was an arrogant, unpleasant individual with whom the jury at his subsequent trial had no empathy. He was hanged at Strangeways Prison, Manchester on 12 May 1936.

Neither, in the case of Joan Wolfe, was there a need for a house-to-house search in which hundreds of coppers would ask 'Have you seen this woman?' wearing down shoe leather and tempers in equal quantities. They knew who she was. All they had to know now was the answer to one question – how did she come to die in Houndown Wood, her head smashed to a pulp?

The Joint Surrey force's Chief Constable called in Chief Inspector Edward Greeno from Metropolitan Headquarters at Scotland Yard to lead a murder enquiry on 8 October. Contrary to popular fiction, 'the Yard' is not always called in to murder cases; neither do its officers have any particular jurisdiction over the local force. The point was, however, that a murder victim in leafy Surrey was a rarity, even in wartime. It was the Yard and 'Murder Squad' men like Greeno who had the experience that mattered.

Molly Lefebure, who admits to being easily over-awed by 'famous detectives', especially from the Yard, had met Greeno in the spring of 1942.

> 'More than anything he resembled a huge, steel-plated battle cruiser, with his jaw thrust forward instead of a prow. He spoke little, noticed everything and was tough, not in the Hollywood style, but genuinely, naturally, quietly, appallingly so.'

Photographs show him as square and solid, with the *de rigeur* trilby, herringbone coat and cigarette.

She had come across him during a post-mortem in Shoreditch Mortuary.

> 'The grim light of battle glimmered in his eyes and he started asking questions in a rather rasping voice that sent shivers down my spine. He was on the warpath and I thought "God help the poor fool he's after."'

She found herself quoting Hilaire Belloc on the lion – 'but it did just as well for Mr Greeno:

> His eyes they are bright
> And his jaw it is grim,
> And a nice little child,
> Will not play with him.'

Edward Greeno retired from the Metropolitan Police in 1960 with the rank of Chief Superintendent and an MBE to his credit. His Parthian shot was the book *War on the Underworld* in which he is proud to have been part of the team of all ranks that was the Met. He enjoyed a yarn over a pint with his sergeants, the confidence of Commissioners at the Yard and never had a driver – 'that oddly named "uniformed constable in plain clothes" – who was not welcome in my home as a guest.'

Addicted to the race course, Greeno was commended eighty-eight times by judges, magistrates and Commissioners. With an ego even larger than the man, he claims to have solved twelve top murder investigations. No doubt, that of Joan Wolfe is among them but I have to claim that the Chief Superintendent's total ought to read eleven.

Greeno was asked to join the CID in 1923 by the man he believed to be the greatest detective of all time, Frederick Wensley, a Dorset man more at home with the denizens of the East End than the cramped corridors of the Yard. In 1928 he was 'lent' to the newly created Flying Squad or 'Sweeney', a motorized unit designed to combat an increasingly sophisticated underworld of the Metropolis.

Promotion to Detective Chief Inspector in 1940 put him on the rota of murder cases and made him a member of the 'Murder Squad', which, as Greeno admits, has never existed by that name.

Although he claimed to suspect *everybody* in his cases, other admissions by Greeno in his book indicate that he was a very narrow policeman and probably not worthy of Molly Lefebure's awe. We might expect that a hard-bitten copper who has seen too much tragedy as a result of murder would believe that killers 'should always – or nearly always – hang', but his belief that murderers *always* return to the scene of their crime is not only naïve and clichéd, it was to have disastrous effects on the man in the frame for Joan Wolfe's murder.

Sir Norman Kendal, Assistant Commissioner at the Yard in charge of CID, sent Greeno down to Surrey on 8 October to 'see what it was all about.'

There was an accommodation problem: 'no room at the inn' for Greeno and Detective Sergeant Frederick Hodge. It occurred to Greeno that the local hostelries, swamped as they were with servicemen, were worried about their time keeping and licensing hours. Greeno sent Hodge out with the message that they weren't worried about this, 'and tell them I'm not a teetotaller either'. Landlord Dick Snow was then able to provide excellent rooms, though in which pub these were and whether it was in Thursley, Witley or Godalming, Greeno doesn't say.

Together, he and Webb organized an extensive search of the woods on the edge of Hankley Common; sixty caped coppers, walking slowly in long lines, elbow to elbow, turning every leaf, prodding every bush, mud caked on their size elevens. In the burial mound itself, Sergeant Ballard, the first policeman called to the scene, found, on 12 October, a tooth, a piece of skull and a tuft of hair. Later the same day, he found a girl's left shoe and, about 90 feet away, the right. Simpson conjectured that, because the shoes were missing and because the girl had scratches on her legs and ankles, she had been killed elsewhere and dragged uphill to the spot where she had been found.

12 October proved a field day for finds associated with the dead girl. A canvas bag containing a rosary and a piece of soap was found next, then a water-bottle, across a stream and up a hill, some twenty yards beyond the left shoe. On the 15th the most crucial find of all – an identity card and National Health Insurance card in the name of Joan Pearl Wolfe. Bingo!

It was perhaps fortunate for the murder team that Joan was killed in wartime. A country under threat of invasion, obsessed with the Fifth Column and convinced that 'careless talk costs lives', insists that its citizenry carry an armoury of personal details that no one would dream of carrying in peacetime. That day, too, Ballard and his constables found a religious tract and a piece of paper, on which was written 'Proposed wife, date and place of birth'. There was also a green purse and, scattered near it, as though emptied perhaps in a violent tussle, its probable contents – a white elephant mascot, a crucifix and a small copy of the New Testament. This and a letter dated 24 August – the Moon Young Ducks Begin to Fly – were the sole belongings of Joan Pearl Wolfe.

More ominously, while Ballard was retrieving the dead girl's personal effects, Constable Joseph Armstrong stumbled upon the bough that killed her, partially covered by growing grass. It lay in Houndown Bottom, measured 1¾ inches across and 38½ inches long and had mousy hairs clinging to one end of it. It had been shaped at both ends. The police photograph of the weapon produced later at the trial makes it clear that the instrument was a silver birch branch. Joan's hair is still clearly seen wedged into the peeling bark. Simpson examined it microscopically and found eight of the dead girl's hairs intact. They had recently been bleached like those still on her head.

On the 18th, Armstrong and Sergeant Wade of the Canadian Army Military Police, stationed at nearby Witley Camp, found the remains of a makeshift shack, constructed of birch saplings. It was at the rear of the officers' lines at Witley Camp just off the Portsmouth road. On the floor they found a luggage ticket, a hairpin, a torn label marked 'Canadian Red Cross' and fragments of a letter.

One of the potential mistakes in the police search came to light later and only through the honesty of the officer concerned. Sergeant James Smith had been with Ballard when he found the bag with the soap and rosary. He also found a knife, but at that stage, it was not apparent to the rank and file of the Surrey constabulary that a knife was involved and he threw it away. This careless officer was luckier than he deserved to be. Greeno says that Smith intended to clean up the knife for gardening use, but when he realized it was too rusty, he discarded it. Sir Norman Kendal rang Greeno to find out what he intended to do about this. 'Nothing,' Greeno said, impressed apparently by the man's honesty. The fact was that incompetence like this could have cost Greeno the case. It seems that Smith was particularly careless because he at first threw the bag away too and 'another officer' (presumably Ballard?) recovered it. No amount of re-searching, even with a mine detector, found that knife again.

As October wore on and the nights drew in, the police dragnet widened. Constable Brian Gunning crossed the road by Dye House and climbed to the old cricket pavilion which stared across the green to the village of Thursley. Here he found a pair of stockings, a black elastic garter, four pieces of sacking and a knitting instruction booklet.

From these sad and scattered remains, Ted Greeno had to reassemble an entire life, one that had lasted for nineteen or twenty years and had come to an abrupt end in a lonely hollow in Houndown Wood.

M. J. TROW

2

There Was a War On

'I am speaking to you from the Cabinet Room at 10 Downing Street. This morning the British Ambassador in Berlin handed the German Government a final note stating that, unless we heard from them by eleven o'clock that they were prepared at once to withdraw their troops from Poland, a state of war would exist between us. I have to tell you now that no such undertaking has been received, and that consequently this country is at war with Germany.'

Many ordinary British people, huddled silently around their valve wirelesses on that Sunday, 3 September 1939, must have asked the same question that one of Alan Bennett's characters poses in *Forty Years On*: 'What have we got to do with Poland?'

The answer was, not a great deal. It was a country that had been partitioned and sold down the river more often than the parson preached about. The point was, however, that for the west of Europe, Britain and France in particular, Poland represented a last straw. In search of *Lebensraum* and territorial aggrandisement on an unprecedented scale, Adolf Hitler ordered his Panzer divisions into the Polish corridor to join East Prussia to the rest of his invincible, eternal Third Reich. In so doing he gave himself six years to live and the world a legacy which only the centuries may one day erase.

In Britain, it was the start of the 'phoney or bore war' – a time of waiting and of false alarms. German civilians, whose army was actually on the offensive but well beyond their own frontiers, called it *Sitzkrieg* (armchair war) and the French, the old enemy, *drôle de guerre* (the funny war). When the deadly Blitzkrieg tactics of Stukas in the air and Panzers on the ground carved a bloody path through the Low Countries and France, it ceased to be a joke. We remained unhit, like a prize fighter waiting for the first punch. It came soon enough, with the thrust of Guderian's *Wehrmacht* through the forest of the Ardennes, batting aside the unfinished Maginot Line and driving for the coast. Paris fell and a numbed, bedraggled and exhausted British Expeditionary Force fell back to Dunkirk where a fortuitous combination of gallant little boats from the south of England and a curious lull in the German advance combined to allow thousands of them to fight another day.

Even before that, panic struck. In August 1939 five people were killed and nearly fifty injured when a bomb exploded in Broadgate, Coventry. Thirty-five shop fronts were shattered, cars were over-turned. That city, so soon to witness devastation on such a scale that its very name became part of the English language, was the victim of the IRA, hovering, as it had done since its creation, to wreak terrible revenge on innocent people because they had the misfortune to be English.

By the end of the month, the lessons of the town of Guernica in Spain and Warsaw in Poland were being taken to heart here too. Shortly before dawn on that last August day, the cities saw a little exodus of wide-eyed, sleepy children, shivering with excitement and incomprehension. Hitler was like some terrible Piper, luring the children out of their homes and into the mountains for a better life. Each of them clutched belongings – a favourite toy, sandwiches, toothbrush, comb, handkerchief, the already ubiquitous (and pointless) gas mask. The country people who took them in were shocked to find so many of them undernourished and covered in rat and flea bites. 'Pick-your-evacuee' sessions were a little like black slave auctions in America's Deep South – the most miserable specimens were left till last. Anyone with a spare room was expected to take them in, however inappropriate that fostering might be. So crusty old bachelors and fussy old spinsters found themselves coping with lice, scabies, impetigo and bed-wetting. In exchange, they got a meagre sum from the government and the knowledge, at least, that they were doing their bit. The feeling of perplexity was mutual – most of these children had never seen a cow before. One London child wrote to his mother: 'They call this Spring, Mum, and they have one down here every year.' The schools became the embarkation points, buses conveying hundreds of children to main-line stations. In London seventy-two underground stations were commandeered to cope with the flow. By the end of that first week, one and a half million 'townies' were experiencing country life for the first time. On the whole, despite binds of affection that grew up, the 'evacuation experience' was not a success and the kids began to drift back.

There was panic, too, in the corridors of power. The War Cabinet of Neville Chamberlain, hopelessly out of his depth in his least fine hour, was given sweeping new powers, unthinkable in peacetime. The armed forces were mobilized and reservists called up. The Coronation Chair from Westminster Abbey joined art treasures from the British Museum on their way to undisclosed destinations – some said an old, abandoned quarry in North Wales – for safe-keeping.

Half an hour after Chamberlain's announcement to a breathless nation, the wail of air-raid sirens could be heard across the capital. It was a false alarm, like the 'phoney war' itself and nothing happened.

By the end of that first month, a kind of routine had emerged. Income tax had risen to its highest ever figure of 7s 6d in the pound – this for a war that would cost Britain £2 million a day to fight. The 100,000 casualties expected in the first weeks had not materialised and the cardboard coffins ready for the firestorm were not used. The only bombardment came from the government, national and local, that seemed kicked into action by fear. Thousands of 'little Hitlers' sprang up in all directions, in every conceivable walk of life, telling people what to do 'if the Invader comes'. To our generation, they are exemplified by the strutting, ineffectual Captain Mainwaring of television's *Dad's Army*, portrayed by Arthur Lowe. A blackout was rigidly enforced. Thick curtains became the order of the day, cardboard shields were fitted over car headlights. Bollards and pavement kerbs were painted white to enable motorists to see and male pedestrians were encouraged to let their shirt tails hang out to avoid accidents after dark. Even so, deaths and accidents on the roads doubled by 1940. Everywhere there were men with blue overalls and tin hats painted with the initials ARP shouting 'Put that bloody light out!' and huge posters, carefully designed by the new Ministry of Information, urged the great British public to save, buy War Bonds, dig for victory. Was their journey really necessary, asked the posters. And they carried a warning too. Britain was alive, it was believed, with a 'fifth column' of spies. 'Careless Talk Costs Lives.' 'Keep It Dark.' 'Walls Have Ears.' 'Keep It Under Your Hat.' 'Be Like Dad – Keep Mum.' The CID in London interned 6,000 aliens in one month alone – the Germans, Austrians and later the Italians who had the misfortune to be born in the wrong country. Ice-cream parlours all but disappeared.

Then came privations. From December 1939 butter and bacon were rationed. The weekly allowance became four ounces of butter, twelve of sugar, four of bacon or ham. Meat was rationed from March 1940; tea, jam, cooking fat and cheese from July. The British public could enjoy the delights of one egg a fortnight. It was a time of making do. The government's Ministry of Food produced recipes every bit as utility as the clothes and the furniture. 'War and Peace' pudding from Canada was a Christmas treat. In the absence of dried fruit, people put diced carrot into Christmas puds. Carrot croquette and carrot fudge were frequent suggestions for the weekly diet, and lest the public think the government was a little obsessive about carrots, All Clear Sandwiches and Woolton Pies were available (proving the government's obsession with parsnips).

Bread was not rationed, perhaps because the folk memory of the people was too long. Bread had been the staple diet for centuries. Times were tough enough as it was. Ration bread and you'd cause a stampede. Even so, the 'British loaf' was coarse in quality, grey in colour and not very appealing. 'British restaurants' sprang up to rival Joe Lyons' Corner Houses, where workers could get a good, cheap meal. Looming large on the menu were ... parsnips and carrots.

Children got the best of it – daily milk and orange juice, even if the latter had little circles of revolting cod liver oil floating on top of it. Against this dietary background, the tinned Spam and dried eggs that came from America under the lease-lend programme may well have seemed like a little taste of heaven.

Nor were privations confined to food. While the Ministry of Agriculture pressured people into replacing begonias with carrots and parsnips, thereby digging for victory, aluminium pots and pans were being collected to remould into aircraft parts. Bones were carefully saved and boiled down into the glue that helped hold those parts together. Railings from parks and gardens became bits of tanks and battleships. After the introduction of clothing coupons in June 1941, trousers appeared without turn-ups and without the extra cloth fashionable in the 'Oxford Bags' of the '30s. Skirts lost their pleats; hemlines got shorter. An ersatz mentality prevailed. Deprived of lipstick, girls painted their lips with beetroot juice. Deprived of stockings – silk was used for parachutes and barrage balloons, and nylons effectively had to wait to be brought over by the Americans – girls coloured their legs with gravy browning and got a friend to draw a seam up the back with an eyebrow pencil.

Queuing (originally – and astonishingly – a French custom) became a national pastime, perhaps even obsession. The joke went that women were physically incapable of walking past a line of people without joining the end of it. An estimated one million of them queued for hours every day, often carrying newspapers to wrap whatever they were buying because paper was in short supply. At the end of it, they would lean over and whisper to their friendly neighbourhood grocer, 'AUC? – Anything Under the Counter?

We were now 'Fortress Britain', isolated from Europe by the sheer speed and success of Hitler's advance. And as if to counter this, to prove to Germany – and to ourselves – that it was 'business as usual', the London theatres reopened after an initial closure. Emlyn Williams starred in *The Corn is Green* and John Gielgud in *Hamlet*. Elsewhere, the furious '40s had replaced the more staid entertainment of pre-war England; Ivor Novello's *Dancing Years* moved over at Drury Lane to ENSA, the Armed Forces Entertainers – known to most as 'Every Night Something Awful'. Gracie Fields and George Formby became its biggest stars. And the Royal Opera House, Covent Garden, became a dance hall.

The radio became an indispensible part of everyday life; not only was it a vital outlet for the Ministry of Information and such war news as the government thought it suitable to release – the nine o'clock news on the BBC's Home Service was essential listening – it also produced conscious and unconscious propaganda which went a long way to bolster public morale. For children, the kindly voice of Derek McCulloch, 'Uncle Mac' – 'Hello, children, everywhere' – had a comforting effect for years after the war was over. For adults, the show of the decade was unquestionably ITMA (It's That Man Again) starring Tommy Handley. Its catchphrases – 'Can I do you now, sir?' and 'I don't mind if I do' – became part of the language. So popular was this programme that it was said that if Hitler invaded on a Thursday night between half past eight and nine o'clock, he'd meet no resistance at all. For the troops, in barracks and camps up and down the country, the Forces Programme, first produced in February 1940, provided twelve hours of light entertainment whose biggest property by far was the Forces' Sweetheart, Vera Lynn. On a slightly more highbrow level 'The Brains Trust' was set up where a panel of experts would answer imponderables of the type that might pop up in those barracks and camps.

If it was highbrow you wanted, Londoners at least could go to one of Henry Wood's Promenade Concerts at the Queen's Hall or listen to lunchtime piano recitals by Dame Myra Hess in the National Gallery, now that all the pictures had gone.

Those with gramophones could invest in the thick plastic records that revolved at 78 revolutions per minute to the strains of 'Any Gum, Chum?' or (the war's all-time favourite) 'Lili Marlene', a British version of a German song heard in North Africa. The song of 1940-41 was undoubtedly 'A Nightingale Sang in Berkeley Square', but rationing produced its own humour on plastic – 'Yes, We Have No Bananas'. As far as silly songs went, however, the world would have to wait until 1944 for the incomparable 'Mairzy Doats and Dozy Doats'.

It was the cinema that provided the biggest escapism. Between 25 and 30 million tickets were sold each week and the queues formed – again – outside the Majestic and the Bijou and the Regal, to watch Clark Gable not giving a damn about Vivienne Leigh and Noël Coward being undeniably fine in the propagandist *In Which We Serve*. No doubt they rolled in the aisles in 1942 when an amazingly earnest and cocksure Errol Flynn in *Desperate Journey* said, 'Now for Australia and a crack at those Japs!'

It was a strange country and a strange time. In January 1940 two million men between the ages of nineteen and twenty-seven were called up, the buff envelope dropping on the morning mat. It was the coldest winter on record – and two more nearly as bad were to follow. The Thames froze as it had not since 1888 when the Ripper struck an added chill to London's heart. Six million people eked out their coal supplies and shivered to the adenoidal drawl of William Joyce on their wireless sets – 'Germany calling, Germany calling.'

In April 1940, Denmark fell. Then the Netherlands. Then Belgium. Chamberlain's feeble 'Hitler has missed the bus' sounded hollow against all of that. Postage went up to 2½d for a standard letter, but at least unemployment dropped to below one million – and after the slump of the '30s, that was no mean achievement.

On 10 May Winston Churchill was called by the King, George VI, to head a new coalition government. His finest hour was at hand, after decades of abuse and cold-shouldering. Men muttered at street corners as they began their new ten-hour factory shifts under the regime of Ernest Bevin, the Minister of Labour. Churchill was the man who had buggered up the Dardenelles, wasn't he? The bloke who sent the troops into unemployed Tonypandy? Still, he was better than Halifax, his rival. And a thousand times better than the discredited Chamberlain, who was to die the following November of cancer, unmissed, unmourned.

By 14 June, Paris had fallen and German jackboots crunched under the Arc de Triomphe. Hitler insisted that the French sign an armistice in the very railway carriage where Field Marshal Foch had received the German surrender in November 1918. He even sat in Foch's chair. There was real relish in that – the old enemy beaten at last.

'Let us brace ourselves,' said Churchill, 'to our duty and so bear ourselves that if the British Commonwealth and Empire lasts a thousand years men will still say, "'This was their finest hour.'"

The summer of 1940 proved to be just that. As the Channel Islands fell, a hastily improvised 'Home Guard', the Local Defence Volunteers (referred to universally as 'Look, Duck and Vanish'), was cobbled together. 250,000 men between the ages of seventeen and sixty-five enlisted in the first week. It is easy to be patronizing and dismissive of this 'Dad's Army'. Newsreels of the time, designed to impress but possibly achieving the opposite, shows unfit, elderly civilians, drilling with armbands, broom handles and pitchforks. Out of this 'citizens' army', in which local commanders were at first elected democratically, emerged a useful, well-trained and organized force, freeing younger men for more essential tasks. Whatever their keenness, however, one thing was certain. They would have been no match for von Runstedt and his Panzers.

What actually saved Britain was a combination of factors – the 21 miles of the English Channel and the sheer dogged courage of the Royal Air Force. In the dreamy August of 1940, a handful of young men in Spitfires and Hurricanes, took off in the two minutes' warning time from their fighter bases at Tangmere and Biggin Hill and Hornchurch. Herman Goering's bombers and their fighter escorts came in wave after wave but were beaten back. Again it was Churchill who found the words: 'Never in the field of human conflict has so much been owed by so many to so few.'

And so Herman Goering's bombers changed tack and targeted the cities.

It is the blitz which more than any other event sharpens our image of Britain at war. 'This is the historic hour,' said Goering, 'when our air force for the first time delivers its blows right into the enemy's heart.' The attack on London, first delivered by over three hundred bombers on 7 September 1940, was said to be in retaliation for Churchill's ordering of an RAF raid on Berlin. Hitler, who had promised that his city would never be bombed, was furious. More than 2,000 casualties emerged from that first day's bombing, which left the London docks blazing. Buckingham Palace became a casualty in the weeks and months that followed. The Queen said, 'I'm glad we've been bombed. It makes me feel that I can look the East End in the face.' Lesser residences were bombed too, not just in London, but in other major cities, Plymouth, Coventry and Hull bearing the brunt along with the capital. On the night of 14 November the anti-aircraft guns that ringed Coventry began firing at seven fifteen. By three in the morning they fell silent, not because the raid was over, but because they were white hot. Firemen, policemen and ambulance crews worked tirelessly around the clock, clearing rubble, tackling flames, carrying out bodies and patching up the injured. This was total war on a scale never dreamed of by von Clausewitz, the military theorist who had coined the sobriquet 'Blitzkrieg' – lightning war – to help explain Napoleon's tactics in the early nineteenth century. Under the rubble and the burning houses and the shattered lives, signs still said 'Business as Usual'. And a police station, battered by incendiary devices, carried a hoarding saying 'Be good, we're still open.'

It was now that the elaborate precautions of 1939 came into their own. Tin huts, named after Sir John Anderson, Lord Privy Seal and the man in charge of Air Raid Precaution work, had been delivered from the spring of that year, giving the lie to those who complained that we were not ready for the war. They were damp and cramped, but, submerged into people's back gardens, could be life savers. The darkness of the blackout now had some point, even if the traffic accident rate had gone up. It slowed down cars on the road and it slowed down trains, now offering only pin points of eerie blue light even in first-class carriages. The only truly pointless expense of the war was the issue of gas masks, which had to be carried at all times and came in neat, square cardboard boxes. Letter boxes were painted with a special yellow paint that turned red on contact with poison gas. But there was no poison gas. Classes were held in how to detect the various types. One smelt strongly of geraniums. All of them caused irritation and discomfort, some blindness, vomiting and death. But they were never used for real. The terror weapon of the First World War, the creeping green of chlorine or mustard gas, did nor feature this time. Instead, children fell about helpless with laughter at the raspberries they were able to blow by inhaling sharply so that the rubber inflated against their cheeks. Everyone who wore a gas mask was actually breathing in the fumes of an asbestos filter, but in the '40s no one bothered about such niceties. There was a war on.

Greta Briggs wrote of London:

'The bombs have shattered my churches, have torn my streets apart.
But they have nor bent my spirit and they shall not break my heart.

For my people's faith and courage are lights of
London town
Which would still shine in legends though my
last broad bridge were
down.'

Winston Churchill, ever grimmer, ever readier perhaps for
invasion than the propaganda-fed millions, spoke on 4 June of
that year, before the *Luftwaffe* changed targets and strengthened
the nation's resolve:

'We shall defend our island, whatever the cost
may be, we shall fight on the beaches, we shall
fight on the landing grounds, we shall fight in
the fields and in the streets, we shall fight in the
hills: we shall never surrender.'

It was a heroic, almost Arthurian concept of romance and
chivalry. But it had a deadlier, steadier truth. And it worked.

It worked even though by February 1941, the average
British family was living on less than £5 per week. The Ministry
of Labour produced some grim figures. Average weekly
expenditure on rent was 10s 6d, on clothes 9s 4d, on fuel and
light 6s 5d, on food £1 14s 1d. There was a war on. Everybody
drew in their belts and did what they could.

Ernest Bevin encouraged Britain's women to fill auxiliary
jobs in industry, especially munitions.

'I cannot offer them a delightful life. I want
them to come forward in the spirit that they are
going to suffer some inconvenience, but with a
determination to help us through.'

Childminding facilities and nurseries were increased and
strengthened, but only after women took to the streets with
prams demanding war work. Posters appeared extolling the
virtue of life in the factories. The actual incentive was little

enough. An average man earned £3 0s 6d a week: his average wife only £1 18s.

By April 1941, all twenty and twenty-one-year-old women had been registered. They were to be made available to 'do their bit' in a variety of ways. They could work in munitions, aircraft and tank factories, making barrage balloons (as Joan Wolfe nearly did). They could take up nursing, or drive buses and trams, thereby releasing men for the armed forces. They could join the growing army of Civil Defence – by 1941, one in six Air Raid Precaution wardens was a woman. They could work for fifty hours as part of the Land Army, in corduroy breeches and slouch hats, weeding, muck-raking, harvesting, rat-catching. They could join the more glamorous back-up units to the armed forces – the WRNS, the WAAF, the ATS. Posters were even produced showing how chic a girl could look in a field cap or even a tin hat.

In factories, the headscarf, tied in front like a turban, not only kept long hair out of eyes and machinery, it became almost a symbol of emancipated womanhood. Women got used to the bad language, the off-colour jokes, the innuendo, a long time before sexual harassment was invented. 'Music While You Work' played happily above the roar of machines in 8,000 factories each day.

On 11 May 1941, the worst night of the London blitz occurred. Losing too many aircraft by day, the *Luftwaffe* now made regular night raids, taking pot luck with radar and the probing fingers of the Ack-Ack battery searchlights. 550 planes dropped over 100,000 incendiary bombs. Every major railway station was hit, as was St Paul's Cathedral, Westminster Abbey and the Houses of Parliament. Churchill was photographed the next morning in the smoking rubble, cigar clamped defiantly between upraised fingers. London, like all the other cities, could take it. 'The V sign,' explained the Prime Minister, 'is the symbol of the unconquerable will of the occupied territories and a portent of the fate awaiting the Nazi tyranny.'

So annoying did the V sign become to the Germans, who found it daubed on walls by partisans all over Europe, that they adopted it themselves, claiming that it was a German idea all along. But then, they had also claimed that Shakespeare was a German . . .

The fate awaiting Nazi tyranny was assuming more realistic proportions by the end of 1941. Breaking the Nazi-Soviet Pact which Hitler had signed with Joseph Stalin to allow him a free hand in Poland, the Führer had now sent his Panzers into the USSR. Like Napoleon before him, his advance collapsed before the terrible Russian winter and the Red Army's dogged defence of its cities was the grimmest the *Wehrmacht* had to face. On 7 December at the naval base of Pearl Harbor, the Americans lost, in just under two hours, five battleships, fourteen frigates, 200 aircraft and nearly 2,500 personnel. Only the lucky absence of their aircraft carriers on manoeuvres had prevented a total catastrophe. The war for the Pacific, between the USA and Britain on the one hand and Japan on the other, was destined to become bigger than that. The most powerful country in the world had been slapped in the face. She wouldn't forget and she wouldn't forgive.

'It is not the end,' said Churchill the following year, the year that Joan Wolfe died. 'It is not even the beginning of the end. But perhaps it is the end of the beginning.'

Molly Lefebure's war was part of all this, yet different. She was astonished when the soon-to-be-legendary Dr Simpson tapped her on the shoulder in Walthamstow cemetery and suggested she be his secretary. He can't have been so astonished when she refused, politely of course. But by three that afternoon she'd changed her mind and a fortnight later became the first secretary (at least the first female on) to set foot in a mortuary – the one at Southwark, where the old Marshalsea Prison had stood before they demolished it in 1887. Because Simpson was attached to Guy's, much of Miss Lefebure's experience was London-based. But he was also Medico-Legal Adviser to the Surrey constabulary (hence his involvement in the case of Joan Wolfe) and from time to time he was called out to other parts of the country too.

It is worth remembering that London, in common with most other cities, was still essentially Victorian in 1942. In fact, cynics have said that the *Luftwaffe* did us an oblique favour by demolishing so much derelict and substandard property, sweeping away in a night's work what was left of the rookeries and tenements of the East End. Molly Lefebure paints a depressing picture of one of these – Berkshire Buildings in Bethnal Green:

'The tenements were arranged on a system of tiers of corridors connected by staircases open on every landing to the small balconies, which no doubt were designed to keep the buildings ventilated but which mainly succeeded in sweeping the place with perishing, dust-whirling draughts. The staircases were dark and their stone steps were worn by many, many weary feet. There was a great smell of rotting plaster, human dirt, latrines, cooking and damp. The staircase and corridor walls were adorned with chalk sketches and scrawls of all kinds, from the harmlessly jocular to the indecent. The buildings echoed with footsteps, babies crying, dishes clattering and radios playing. Silence was obviously unknown there.

'The blocks were each four storeys high with a kind of penthouse communal laundry under the roof. Here were long-stained sinks and fixed clothes lines. On each floor . . . was a lavatory, which . . . served all the flats on that floor, and a washroom with a very dirty sink – there were no bathrooms . . . None of the flats had running water; all water had to be fetched for the washrooms.

'The lavatories and washrooms were filthy, stinking places, their doors swinging wide open to the corridors, up and down which the stinks wafted freely.'

And when CKS was called to a suicide in south London, Molly Lefebure took in the surroundings:

> '... from the once green-papered walls – now blotchy and peeling with damp, so that they appeared to be suffering from some ghastly skin disease, as did the lumped, clotted and pitted surface of the filthy ceiling – to the squat, slow, fat bug which was taking a trip along a crack by the fireplace. In one dark corner was a wooden table, spread with an old sheet of newspaper, and on this stood a filthy mug, some pieces of twisted cutlery and a tin plate heaped with fragments of cold potato and cabbage in congealed gravy. By the table was a rag-strewn chair and an old trunk. On a second table stood a pile of dusty gramophone records and an old portable gramophone. There was a small bedside stand with all sorts of filthy odds and ends on it, and beneath this was an unspeakable bucket which had been used for everything from chamber-pot to scrap-bin and which had obviously mot been emptied for several days ... This was the 'home' of a Londoner in the year 1943.'

London was, however, as Miss Molly points out, a 'schizophrenic' city. It had its brighter side, if you had the money and knew where to go. Simpson takes up the story:

> 'I used to meet my two London contemporaries, Francis Camps and Donald Teare, regularly at the French restaurant L'Etoile in Charlotte Street, where good food

and wine were still available in spite of shortages and rationing. Nino, the proprietor, had devised a substitute for the dry Martinis and Pernods of peacetime, a powerful aperitif which he called "ARP" ... which consisted of absinthe, rum and paregoric – or so Nino said.'

It was here that the three pathologists would talk shop, along, sometimes, with Eric Gardner, chauffeur-driven from Surrey in a 'sleek blue Railton', a 'Rolls Royceish' sort of vehicle the Met used as squad cars, though in the inevitable black. When a fifth colleague, Dr Grace, Home Office Pathologist in Liverpool and Chester, joined them, they would decamp to the Eastern Hotel, convenient for his last train home. The problem was that the staff here took too much notice of air-raid sirens and there wasn't the privacy to 'produce a piece of bloodstained clothing or a mangled larynx, or even the latest "filthy" pictures of some new crime we wished to show each other.'

It was in this hotel in the summer of 1941 that Simpson and Gardner entered the same gents' cubicle for CKS to prove his point about self-strangulation using a double knot. The sudden tautening of the stocking turned Simpson's face blue and his vision swam. Luckily, Gardner loosened the ligature in time, or the next day's headlines, Simpson conjectured, might have read 'Mystery of Home Office Pathologist's sudden death; two in locked men's toilet at London hotel.'

There was a sense of frustration for men whose occupation had essentially nothing to do with wartime. Routes had to be changed because of bomb craters and burst mains. Courtroom procedures were disrupted – as when Hervey Wyatt, the Southwark coroner, adjourned his proceedings by means of a trap-door to the safety of an underground cellar during an air raid. The war also produced a lot more work. Molly Lefebure, less absorbed surely than Simpson, noticed the war weariness:

'One would feel a bout coming on, endeavour to fight it off, fall victim to it, shiver and shake in its grasp, finally to emerge from it bored, depressed and listless. It was a real illness … and as the war went on, almost everybody fell victim to it … Some it made drink a lot. Others took to bed – with others – a lot. Some became hilariously gay, brave and hearty. Others became sardonic and bored. Some seriously depressed. The Cockneys sharpened their celebrated wit until it had an edge which cut as painfully and bitterly as grass. A few took to prayer …'

And a few took to crime. In 1939 over 300,000 crimes of all types were reported in England and Wales. By the end of the war in 1945, the figure was 475,000 – an increase of 60 per cent. Crime figures are notoriously difficult to handle. The classic example came from the '30s when Lord Trenchard, the then new Metropolitan Police Commissioner, ordered a new method of recording crime – 'crimes reported' and 'suspected stolen' figures were kept in one book. The larceny figures for 1931 therefore stand at 9,534 for the area served by the Met and an unbelievable 34,783 for the start of 1932! Without a careful study of Trenchard's system, however, the historian and sociologist might well see this as a real and astronomic crime increase created, say, by the economic viciousness of the slump.

In wartime, however, the crime increase is marked. Because of a shortage of newsprint, the plethora of war news and the need, underlined by a Ministry of Information every bit as attuned to the requirements of propaganda as that of Josef Goebbels in Germany, to keep morale high, crime was not reported. Even so, local, inexperienced newshounds yapped around Greeno, pestering him at lunch during his investigations. One went so far as to impersonate him to get more information. Bearing in mind that the *Daily Express*'s crime reporters regarded the solving of the murder of Joan Wolfe as the best example of detection of the century, its coverage at the time was minimal. This is not surprising against rival news like Dieppe and El Alamein. In *The Ministry of Fear*, written in 1942, Graham Greene sums it up in a nutshell: 'Nobody troubled about single deaths … in the middle of a daily massacre'. The actual number of murders showed little variation in the war years. There were 135 in the first year of the war; 141 in the last. Interestingly, the 'record' year was 1942, with 159 known cases. Other forms of crime proliferated – woundings nearly doubled, theft rocketed. Rationing created the spiv and the black marketeer – war profiteers who were determined to cash in on the peculiarities of the hour. And this sort of crime was regarded rather as we regard parking on a double yellow line today, or as our ancestors regarded smuggling in the eighteenth century – no crime at all. So, perfectly honest, law-abiding citizens indulged in it, making the job of the police all the more difficult.

Simpson sums up the motive for all this increased crime succinctly:

'Emergency regulations, uniforms, drafting, service orders and a life of discipline cramp the freedom of many young men and during the long periods of wartime training and waiting not a few of them got bored – "browned off" was the common term. Some missed their wives or girlfriends and got into trouble with local girls and camp followers … urged on by long periods of sex starvation. So during the "phoney" and training periods of 1939-43 there was a steady flow of rapes (some with strangling and other violence), of assaults (some fatal), of abortions and infanticides, of breaking into "deserted" houses (sometimes with violence), all arising from the changes in life that were thrust by service conditions on ordinary people.'

This was the first war to involve a genuine citizens' army, in which men, women and children were in the front line. And it took its toll. If camaraderie increased and the resolve to survive stiffened, then so too life became cheap. People lived for today, because tomorrow . . . well, you never knew. If shop fronts have been smashed by bombs, why not help yourself to the window display? If you can't get cigarettes or stockings or chocolate, why not buy then from that bloke on the corner? The one with the natty 'tache and the outsize trench coat? And if you're of a certain disposition, why not have that tart in the alleyway? She won't cost much, and God knows when you'll have the chance again. So the litany begins: Leading Aircraftsman Arthur Heys strangled WAAF Winnie Evans at an aerodrome in Suffolk; Samuel Morgan killed fifteen-year-old Mary Hagan in a Liverpool blockhouse; Harold Hill strangled and stabbed two little girls in a field in Buckinghamshire – and left his gas mask behind; officer cadet Gordon Cummins killed and mutilated four women in London, giving rise to memories of the Ripper and, incidentally, being caught by Ted Greeno; and, although it was not to come to light until after the war, John Reginald Halliday Christie was making good use of his back garden at 10, Rillington Place.

And as if we didn't have enough problems of our own, the Americans and Canadians were 'overpaid, over-sexed and over here'.

Canada, as part of the Commonwealth and a former part of the Empire, entered the war in 1939 with a tiny armed strength – 4,500 soldiers, 4,000 airmen and a navy of seventeen ships.

The commonly held belief that the former Empire would join the war as it had in 1914 because there was 'one king, one flag, one cause', was not necessarily true. Canada was a Dominion and had been since 1870. It had in effect seventy years of independence from the mother country and its ethnic white community – the French or Quebecois – had never entirely felt at one with British Imperialism. It is not true to assert however that it was the French antipathy that led to a three-day debate in the Ottawa Parliament before Canada decided to join Britain's war. Literally from 3 September 1939, the day Britain declared war on Germany and four days before the Ottawa Parliament met, Governor-General Mackenzie Kind placed the armed forces on a war footing, having already, on 25 August, advised the various military districts to 'adopt precautionary stage against Germany'. The British navy could use Canadian ports and Nazi sympathizers were already being rounded up. The only idea at which Ottawa balked – and which was ultimately decided by a plebiscite – was the notion of conscription for overseas service.

When adopted in 1943, conscription raised the total of combatants to 675,564 men under arms, with 45 operational air squadrons and 373 naval vessels. The first Canadian troops arrived in this country on 17 December 1939, the Moon in which the Young Fellow Spreads the Brush, many of them destined to be stationed in and around Surrey and Hampshire. Typically, Churchill jumped the gun. The idea was to announce the arrival of the troops to the Canadian people first, two days after they landed. In the event, Churchill leaked the information to the British people on the 18th without consulting the Canadians. Luckily, they had a forgiving nature. The people of Canada were to experience a watered-down version of the 'fortress' problems of Britain. There was light rationing, with alcohol and rubber (for car tyres) in the shortest supply. Posters said 'Use It Up, Wear It Out, Make It Do and Do Without', but at the same time the well-resourced Dominion was a huge supplier to Britain of men, ships, aircraft, weapons and food. They included some 10,000 Americans who had crossed the border into Canada to enlist in a war that was, as yet, strictly none of their business. No doubt many of these troops shared the views of one of the Eagle Squadron, Americans flying with the RAF, that 'we were tired of hanging around the corner drugstore at home … Didn't you ever hear of a kid running away from home to join the circus?'

The advent of the Americans – the first officially ashore was private Milburn H Henke from Minnesota on 26 January 1942 – over-shadowed the Canadian input. At once more ebullient and more colourful (not to say richer), the GIs provided 'candy', nylon stockings and excitement. And there was no shortage of local girls who would cram themselves into the liberty buses (called 'passion wagons') to carry them to dances at the nearest air force or army camp. The jokes about these girls were legion – 'Have you heard about the new utility knickers? One Yank and they're off!'

Before the war, it was highly unusual to see a woman alone in a pub or at a dance. The arrival of the war, the GI and the jitterbug changed all that. The latest dance craze that was sweeping America caused some dance hall proprietors to ban it to protect their floors. The big band sound of band leaders like Henry Hall provided the background to a series of whirlwind romances. The marriage rate had already risen from 8.5 to 11.2 per thousand before the Americans/Canadians arrived. There was perhaps no need for the American government to issue leaflets to its troops with this advice:

> 'Don't show off or brag or bluster – "swank" as the British say. Don't make fun of British speech or accents. *Never* criticize the King or Queen … Stop and think before you sound off about lukewarm beer and cold, boiled potatoes …'

… because 80,000 British girls had left the country as GI brides by 1945. As well as offering cigarettes, scented soap and the rest of the goodies from their PX rations, the Americans and Canadians offered romance with its concomitant heartache. The agony columns were littered with letters that started 'I met this man at a dance …'

In the year that Joan Wolfe died, the new promiscuity of the 'live for today, for tomorrow we die' generation was countered by the last lingering vestiges of Victorian morality in just such a letter to *Woman* magazine:

'I am serving in the Forces and find I am going to have a baby. Two men could be responsible, but I don't know which. Both have offered to marry me, but I can't decide which. Would it be better to throw them both over and make a fresh start?

'Much better. You don't love either of them and whoever marries you will never feel sure of you. Get over this trouble, make up your mind to be morally stronger in future and marry when you find a man you can really love; moreover, a man who will respect you before marriage.'

There were many who would ridicule our Allies and resent their presence. Some of them may have given testimony at the trial in the Joan Wolfe case. Others, like the journalist J E Sewell of the *Daily Telegraph* were more impressed. He was writing, it is true, in January 1943, but he is describing the army that had been camped around Witley and Thursley since 1940:

'This was the army which in 1940 and 1941 stood ready to engage Hitler's divisions if they attempted the costly but tempting coup of invasion. The same army is now crouched in his rear, twitching and ready to spring ... [The Canadian soldier] has been trained and retrained. He has done exercise after exercise, in mud and dust, in snow and sunshine, for three years. He has followed the war through the columns of unfamiliar newspapers ... From time to time, though not regularly, he hears from his mother and the girl he wanted to marry; and the most he has seen of the Germans in three years has been the vapour trails in the sky or an occasional sneak raider giving a wide berth to the Bofors batteries around his camp ... In my tour I watched Canadian troops in company and battalion exercises, sometimes with live ammunition, rehearsing yet again the battle drill which would be used if the Nazis ever tried to penetrate our defences ... [The Canadian soldier] is leaping in and out of Bren carriers, firing his three inch mortars across the Downs, creeping through little Sussex ravines with his rifle, sleeping out in the woods on occasions ... some of them are Indian trappers, who teach Canada's townsmen and miners the secrets of the wild that they learned in childhood ... He will be missed when he goes on active service in the offensive yet to come. He has been, and will be, very patient; but he knows that his chance will come, and that, when it comes, he will be perfectly equipped for the job.

All over the heathlands of southern England, watching for the foe who never came. An army-in-being.

At the time Sewell was writing, part of this army had been sacrificed, if that is not too strong a word, on the abortive 'reconnaissance in force' on Dieppe on 19 August 1941. 6,086 men had taken part, including 5,000 Canadians. The result was a disaster. Of the appalling 4,384 casualties, 3,379 were Canadians. At least it taught us the valuable lesson of how *not* to invade Europe.

And after Sewell wrote, the Canadians were to excel themselves. We might expect Colonel Nicholson, the official historian of the Canadian Army, to sing their praises by writing that wherever the Canadians went, the most elite German troops had to be put in against them, but Field Marshal Montgomery praised them too – 'When I say you did magnificently,' he said in Italy to the 1st Infantry and 5th

Armoured Divisions, 'I *mean* magnificently.' When even the German High Command concurred, you've got to start believing it. General von Vietinghoff wrote, '… only Canadians attack like that!'

And the downside of all this chest-thumping? Keith Simpson reminds us: 'Some … got into trouble with local girls and camp followers …'

Camp followers like Joan Pearl Wolfe.

3

Joan Pearl Wolfe

I have two photographs of Joan Wolfe before me. One, courtesy of the *Daily Express* of 1943, shows a fresh-faced, smiling girl with dimples, the unflattering hair-style of the period that tended to make women look older than they really were, and prominent front teeth. The other, from the *Daily Mirror* of the same year, is a full-length snapshot, showing the heavy lace-up shoes, ankle socks and belted dress. The crucifix is in evidence around her neck. She is not smiling, rather squinting into the sun. Perhaps the snap was taken in the summer of '42, when she had only months, or weeks, to live.

Joan was born on 11 March 1923. According to testimony at the trial for her murder, Joan is supposed to have claimed that she was born in Germany. Two people with whom I have been in contact who knew the Wolfe family shortly before and during the war, find this hard to believe. It emerged in casual conversation between Joan and Rudolph Franz Dworsky, a Sudeten German (who was also a Czech national) serving with the Edmonton Regiment, Canadian Army. It is an odd thing for an apparently English girl to claim, especially in wartime. Perhaps she just wanted to put Dworsky at his ease, himself an alien on foreign soil. In any case, the Sudeten-Czech-Canadian couldn't remember the conversation taking place. Joan's mother, Edith, had remarried by the time of the trial of her daughter's murderer and lived at 72 Goods Station Road, one of the less desirable areas perhaps of the fadedly genteel Tunbridge Wells.

Edith Mary Watts had been married three times. The only other child of these unions to be mentioned in letters at the trial was Allan (now dead), but in fact Joan had a sister and a half-sister by a different father. Yvonne was the daughter of Mr Wolfe and Enid the daughter of Mr Wood. One or both of these girls worked in a laundry when they left school. It is not clear after all these years whose child Allan was, but he was always known as Allan Wolfe. Someone who lived nearby at the time remembers that he was an errand boy and famous for his incredible whistling skills.

Messrs Wolfe and Wood died, one by his own hand. I placed a letter in the *Kent and Sussex Courier* asking for information from anyone who remembered Joan. Not surprisingly, perhaps, the immediate family have not come forward and, with three husbands to deal with, the information I did receive from former neighbours is necessarily sketchy. The man assumed to be Mr Wolfe suffered from what everyone believed to be a form of sleeping sickness. His behaviour was certainly peculiar. In a town much smaller than it is today, where everybody knew everybody else, Mr Wolfe was a familiar character in Tunbridge Wells, wandering the streets with his hands suddenly flailing in the air. In the absence of evidence to the contrary, I must assume that this was the man, exhausted and confused, who gassed himself, according to his daughter Joan. She carried his photo in her handbag.

Edith Watts remembered her daughter owning Exhibit 25, a green purse. The crucifix – Exhibit 14 at the trial – bears silent witness to Joan's piety. Macdonald Critchley MD, who edited the *Notable British Trials* volume on the case, calls it rather 'religiosity', implying that Joan's religious beliefs were less than skin deep, that she bore the trappings of devotion and believed none of it. For thirteen and a half years, he says, she had been brought up in a strict Catholic convent, although two of my informants from Tunbridge Wells do not remember this.

They both say that she attended, as a teenager at least, the Church of England school then in Stephen Street.

A third however, does, Mrs Betty Holliday's father had a lock-up shop in Crescent Road, Tonbridge, which was taken over by a Mr Wolfe in the year of the General Strike, 1926. The Wolfe family moved to Tunbridge Wells some time later. His daughter Joan did indeed attend a convent school, the uniform of which was brown and red, complete with cloak, lace-up shoes and ankle socks. Betty remembers Joan as a 'real plain Jane' and thought she didn't look any too bright. She believes the convent may have been at Mark Cross in Sussex and this would explain Joan making her way to the station in the company of nuns. She believes that a richer aunt paid for Joan's education, but why she should have been singled out is unclear. Certainly, there were religious overtones about Joan. Her letters, the simple, tragic words she scrawled in the soft wood of Thursley cricket pavilion, her naïvety in a harsh and reeling world – all these give a picture of a nice, respectable, pious girl.

Her behaviour may lead us to believe that she was a nice, respectable, pious girl gone bad.

Mrs Watts does not emerge from her trial evidence as a very caring mother. Her letters to Joan were constantly carping about the girl's lifestyle and betray decades of prejudice, not to mention a classic case of the generation gap. It may be unfair to judge Edith Watts in this way. One of my informants remembers her as a very caring woman, forever gathering waifs and strays under her wing. Perhaps Joan was the last straw and what we see in Edith's letters to her daughter is a mother at her wits' end.

Joan had first left home, according to her mother, when she was sixteen. Mrs Watts had no idea why. She had spoken to Joan about sleeping out all night and keeping late hours – they had long talks about it – but they had not quarrelled over it and Mrs Watts seemed perfectly happy with her daughter's engagement to a young man in Tunbridge Wells. Perhaps it was his car that neighbours noticed turning up for Joan at the

Watts' house in Lodge Oak Lane. Certainly, there was much to stare at – a car outside a council house in 1938 was still a novelty. At the age of sixteen and a half, however, Joan began to 'go with soldiers'. The views of her fiancé are not recorded.

Prejudice against the regular army goes back to its inception in the seventeenth century. Apart from the cost of supporting military units in peacetime, the behaviour of the 'brutal, licentious soldiery' left a great deal to be desired. They drank, they fought and they womanized. They fact that this was 1942 and that a very different kind of man was now in uniform – not one of Wellington's 'scum of the earth, enlisted for drink' but conscripted civilians from all walks of life – made no difference to Edith Watts. Macdonald Critchley refers to Joan by the rather archaic phrase, a 'camp follower': a type of woman more common in Victorian England and earlier, who became 'married' not to a man, but to a regiment. Such women had followed the flag everywhere in the days of Empire, cooking, cleaning, bandaging their menfolk under fire. Their children became, in the fullness of time, soldiers or camp followers themselves. And even in 1942, serving soldiers had to obtain official permission from their commanding officers to marry.

Army towns like Aldershot, Windsor, Brighton, Scarborough, Warminster and of course London attracted a constant flow of these girls. The slur against 'going for [i.e. becoming] a soldier' was great enough for men in the nineteenth century, but their women were regarded as the lowest form of prostitute and the army's constant dread of ever-rampant venereal disease was attributed solely to them. Various contagious diseases acts were passed in an attempt to stem the rising tide. During the First World War it was a crime for an infected woman to communicate it to a member of the armed forces or to solicit him. To those who didn't know the army, little distinction was drawn between the loyal, loving 'women' (who were until well after the turn of the century common law wives) and the prostitutes who hung around the camps, as reliant as the former of soldiers for their next meal ticket.

The existence of a conscripted force increased the likelihood of any teenaged girl meeting soldiers. And we need not speculate on the hackneyed lure of the uniform – although it was a 'selling point' in many recruiting posters before 1914 – and its influence on girls like Joan. A man in uniform represented freedom, escapism, romance. Things too good to be passed up by a convent girl in search of love.

Joan had first gone to Aldershot, the 'home' of the British Army since 1851. A distraught Mrs Watts contacted the police and probation officers and a month later, Joan was brought back by her fiancé's mother. Her own mother never did find out exactly where she had been. We are more able to understand now the motives of the runaway. They are often not as tangible as hating home (although Joan had had not one, but two stepfathers by this time and confessed that she and her mother were 'not friends'). Certainly her behaviour seemed incomprehensible to Edith Watts. By this time the war was well under way and there was an abundance of men in khaki. Joan no longer had to travel to find soldiers – there were several stationed in the Tunbridge Wells area. She broke off her engagement and went to London to train as a storekeeper in an aircraft factory – the most dangerous place in the country outside airfields. 'Doing her bit' lasted a month, although she let her mother believe that the job continued. Mrs Watts discovered from various landladies that the job had long gone and that Joan was drifting. Joan came home again. Mrs Watts insisted that she never quarrelled with the girl – 'I just used to talk to her and point out how wrong it was to keep leaving home and not letting me know where she was and … associating with men. She was much too young …'

At about the end of April 1942, Mrs Watts received a letter from Joan telling her that she was staying at the Quadrant (either Raynes Park or Denmark Hill – there are, according to the A-Z, two Quadrants in London) before drifting into Surrey by way of Reading.

A curious light is shed on Mrs Watts' view of the world in the letter she wrote to Joan on 4 May – the Frog Moon: 'If you have any respect for me or yourself, for God's sake go and get cured.' She assumed her daughter had VD. When Linton Thorp KC asked her at the trial what evidence she had to think this, she put forward the oddly inverted argument that 'someone told me that was probably the reason that she went with all these men, because she was not like it when she was young.' If we take this testimony at face value, it implies that Joan had become that creature of erotic fiction, the nymphomaniac; and if we understand Mrs Watts correctly, her disease somehow gave her a compulsion to sleep with men.

Greeno, having met Mrs Watts and shown her the sad relics of her daughter found scattered in Houndown Wood, is unsympathetic towards the girl:

> '...we began to see almost three dimensionally this pathetic little tramp who was all a bad girl is supposed to be – her own mother suspected that she was diseased. She could not live without sex, but she could be unshakeably faithful to one man while romance lasted ...'

With the next breath, having implied that her daughter was sexually insatiable, Mrs Watts told Thorp that she did not actually know what Joan did with men, but she certainly had a preference for Canadians. Thorp's question was ambiguous – 'As far as you know, had she been going with many men?' The phrase in the '40s meant 'going out with' or, as the Canadians/Americans said, 'dating'. To Mrs Watts, it might have meant something more specific and perhaps she was embarrassed, in the spotlight of the courtroom, to go into details. Two of these Canadians, Kelly Gallagher and the French-Canadian Thomas Bellie, Joan had brought to her mother's house, probably in October 1941. Mrs Watts does not tell us her views on them, but the mere fact that Joan brought them home – one at a time, one gathers – is indicative of an ordinary teenager's desire for her current young man to meet her family.

Betty Holliday remembers the Canadians in the Tunbridge Wells area. At the bottom of the hill opposite the station was a pub with a rather dubious reputation, the Clarendon. The troops, posted in outlying districts, came in by train and made for the hostelry. Was it here that Joan met her two friends?

But the distraught Mrs Watts goes on in a letter read out in court and posted to Joan early in May 1942:

> 'I am finished with you. I have been more than fair to you, forgiven you for things that no other mother would have done. Joan, you have no respect for me or yourself. For God's sake go and get cured [of VD] and make an effort to be a good girl. I will do anything for you if you will help yourself. I am not sending you your Ration Book because I do not want you to stay there. You said something about re-paying me for all that I have done for you. Joan, nothing can re-pay me for that and I do not want re-paying for anything that I have ever done for you, my child. I shall be paid in full the day you come and truthfully say "Mum, I have been cured and I am going to be a good girl." Joan, that will be the happiest day of my life.'

She urged her daughter to think of her little brother Allan and not to let him down as well as her:

> 'When I am dead you will think about all this and wish you had been a better girl to me … Remember remorse is the worst thing in the world to bear … whatever you decide to do think well before you do it – I am still praying for you every night.'

Like many runaways before and since, Joan's character was highly complex and her motives confused. Macdonald Critchley refers to her as 'wayward and depraved and yet at the same time refined, serious, devout'. In some ways she was the classic product of a broken home. Her father had committed suicide by gassing himself, for what precise reason is unknown, and her mother had married again twice. There is no mention of the relationship between Joan and her stepfathers in any surviving correspondence, but the question mark alone may speak volumes and go part of the way to explaining Joan's 'waywardness'.

Joan had apparently spent thirteen and a half years at a convent school, no doubt with its attendant discipline, and had learned fluent French. She had become engaged to a Canadian soldier her mother did not appear to know – Francis Hearn – but the day before she met the man to be accused of her murder, he had sailed for Canada, having promised to marry her. At her trial, it emerged that Joan referred to herself as his wife and she wore the ring he had given her. Like much that she said, it has to be taken with variously sized pinches of salt.

Macdonald Critchley goes into flights of fantasy to explain the convent girl gone bad, pointing out that eroticism is frequently linked with extreme piety and citing the French writer Emile Zola and the English poet Coventry Patmore as expressions of it in literature. He also points out that the 'sexologists' Kraft-Ebbing and Havelock Ellis devote a great deal of space to it and that the English Quakers, German 'Muckers' and American 'Perfectionist Bundlers' provide historical examples of promiscuity and sexuality in a strong bond. The Muckers were a fanatical sect of mystics founded at Konigsberg in 1835 by two Lutheran pastors, Diestel and Ebel. Their members were pledged to a life of higher piety and most of them seem to have been drawn from the ranks of the German aristocracy. Some of their leaders were imprisoned between 1839 and 1842 on charges of immorality involving young girls.

The Perfectionists were established in 1845 by John Humphrey Noyes and they established a religious community at Oneida, New York State. The Bundlers believed that they had reached such a state of grace that sin was impossible for them. In other words, whatever they did was good. They were a community in every sense, sharing goods and wives much in the manner of the short-lived hippy communes of the late 1960s and '70s. They called this 'complex marriage' but it was in fact free love. After 1880, capitalism seems to have hit them in a big way and they became shareholders in the Oneida Community Ltd. How the women were apportioned was not made clear!

To Critchley, then, Joan was 'religious' rather than 'pious'; the wearing of a crucifix and the fear of committing sin which she confided in a letter to her lover are simply the ritualistic trappings of faith without any necessarily concomitant belief. She wrote a prayer to the Virgin Mary on the wooden walls of Thursley cricket pavilion which became a trysting place, even a shrine.

What does Critchley make of the girl's relationships with men? He lumps her into the increasingly large group of 'the teenage sutler [camp follower] who dresses and acts precociously and who is attracted to – or attracted by – a certain type of serviceman.' The problem of course was that there were thousands of servicemen, especially American and Canadian, lonely, miles from home and unsure of their future. Critchley found it difficult to explain, in 1959 when they had long gone home, what the charm of these 'chickens' was. Was it the availability of younger girls, more susceptible to the blandishments of cigarettes, nylon stockings, K Rations and 'other PX treasures'? certainly, Joan relied on her lover for coupons and money in an age of austere wartime rationing. Superintendent Tom Roberts of the Surrey CID reported to his Chief Constable that 'the victim was one of a group of girls who had been regular camp followers of the Canadians. Since they had been encamped at Hankley Common, girls had congregated there from all over England.'

These girls were not the suaver 'Piccadilly commandos' of the West End. An American colonel, perhaps more prudish than most, wrote while on leave in London in 1944:

> 'I think I should tell you that these 'ladies of the night' do not lack for customers, most of whom, I am sorry to say, wear the uniform of the United States Army. It seems that they are in every doorway. They carry small torches so that they can be seen in the blackout and their customers do likewise … They carry on their 'business' in the very shop doorway in which they stand. Once they have struck a "bargain" with their customers, the "service" is performed on the spot in the standing position. In this way, unless the customer demands otherwise, a girl can perform a "service" five times more quickly than in a hotel room … Others of their kind who work the Hyde Park area are known as "rangers".'

There was, of course, nothing new in all this, not even, probably, the numbers. An equally appalled (but privately delighted?) Francis Place, the radical tailor of Charing Cross, was making similar observations 125 years earlier. Only the clients' uniforms were different.

The tragedy of these teenaged girls is that they were actually naïve, easily impressed by the crisp brown and khaki uniforms and the 'Hollywood' drawl, and they were a highly vulnerable target group. Inefficient as prostitutes in an age before effective birth control, they often became pregnant. GIs and Canadians were issued with free contraceptives. An American sergeant announced to his platoon at reveille one morning, 'I'm told we have thirty thousand rubbers in the supply room. I want you people to do something about this.' In Bedford, they floated them down the river, inflated, to impress giggling girls. American condoms were said to have steel tips …

Joan wrote in her letters that she didn't understand men and, in a way, that was pathetically true. Adolescent camp followers like Joan lived rough, infested (as she was) with lice. When similar cases were sent to hospital (as she was) or to remand homes, their hair had often to be shaved, their clothes cut off and burned. She only owned one set of clothes – those in which she died, the shabby green and white frock and shabbier underwear. Whatever became of the clothes her mother referred to in a letter to Joan and had collected from the White swan where she had once stayed, they had gone by the summer of '42. The belt in which she was photographed, possibly in the summer before she died, had become a piece of string by September.

For a time, she lived in the cricket pavilion at Thursley, somewhat derelict not what the war had taken all the young cricketers of the parish. It had a little white-painted veranda fence at the front, a single, glass-paned door and two windows. For an unspecified period in the early autumn of '42, it became Joan's home. On its walls, she left something of herself in a series of writings and drawings. Here was a yacht on the sea, a steamship, birds and a rising sun and the words 'My lover lies over the ocean. Please send him back to me.' There, a dog rose with the legend 'Wild rose of England. Forever. Sept. 1942.' And a childish house without perspective with the sun above it – always the shining sun: 'Our little Grey home in the West.' There were also two verses, redolent of her convent upbringing.

> Oh Holy Virgin in the midst of all thy glory we
> implore thee not to forget
> the sorrows of this world.
> Cast a look of pity
> upon all those who are
> suffering against lifes
> difficulties and who cease not to feel all its

bitterness. Pardon the
weakness of our faith:
Have pity on all those
whom we love. O Holy
Mary show a Mothers
compassion towards the
sorrowful to all who pray and to all who
tremble under life's
afflictions and give them all hope and peace.

The kiss of the sun for pardon
The song of the bird for mirth
One is nearer to God in a garden
Than anywhere else on earth.

Or in a wood perhaps. On the edge of Hankley Common.

Macdonald Critchley divides graffiti into four categories according to social anthropology: the political, the obscene, the self-assertive and the religious. It is to the last two categories that Joan's wall scribbling belong – the mark of the naïve, the young, the lonely, 'with a drive', he writes, 'towards wish-fulfilment.'

What was the greatest wish of Joan Pearl Wolfe? Simply to be loved – arguably for the first time in her life – and it led directly to murder. On the walls of the Thursley cricket pavilion, Joan lovingly doodled the name of her lover: 'A. Sangret. Canada. J. Wolfe now Mrs Sangret. England September 9 1942.' She even gave his age – twenty-eight – and hers – nineteen – and their respective addresses. Perhaps the commonality of names appealed to her – 'Pte A Sangret, Maidstone, Saskatchewan ...' 'Mrs A. Sangret, Tunbridge Wells, Kent ...' And there too was the home they would one day share as real man and wife: 'Our little Grey home in the West.'

4

The Lovers

According to his statement – then the longest in criminal history – and the answers he gave at his subsequent trial for her murder, Private August Sangret of the Regina Rifle Regiment first met Joan Wolfe on the evening of Friday, 17 July 1952, at a pub in Godalming – probably the one opposite the cinema at the top of the hill.

The little town in 'the valley of the nightingales' has now almost been swallowed up by its bigger neighbour Guildford. Mentioned in Domesday, the borough itself is of comparatively late origin, dating from 1575. For long a staging post on the London to Portsmouth road, its High Street still boasts seventeenth century buildings which were in fact coaching inns. Peter the Great, Tsar of all the Russias, dined at the King's Arms Royal Hotel in 1689 while opening his 'window on the West'. The Old Town Hall, built in 1814, is a curious octagonal building of an earlier style and market stall holders traded under its arches. The world's first electric street lamps were switched on here on 26 September 1881.

In the '40s, the town was probably best known for Charterhouse School, which had moved to the area from Sutton in 1872. A typical gazetteer of the early '50s spends longer describing the school than the town:

> 'The buildings include chapel, laboratories, library. The 11 houses accommodate about 650

boys; there are scholarships to the school. Boys may also receive grants according to need, to enable them to continue their education at a university or other institution.'

Burgate stone had long been quarried nearby and the town's chief industries were listed as: drug-making, knitting, malt, corn, leather, paper and cloth, the borough coat of arms depicting a woolsack. Godalming's population in 1951 was 14,244, but a decade earlier that figure was swelled enormously by troops in all shades of khaki and brown, limbering up for the abortive raid on Dieppe and the eventual successful one on the beaches of Normandy.

I visited it on a quiet Sunday in April. The sun threw sharp shadows on the Victorian post office where Joan had collected her mail, the carping, desperate letters her mother sent. The narrow High Street where Allied soldiers strolled rang to the strains of a marching band in scarlet, playing, among other tunes of glory for St George's Day, the oddly unpatriotic 'The United States Marines'.

At about seven o'clock, on that July evening seventy years ago, August Sangret noticed a rather scruffy girl come into the bar. She bought a lemonade and sat near him and he asked her if she couldn't get anything stronger than that. She told him she didn't drink anything stronger. He offered her a cigarette. She told him she didn't smoke. The convent girl had not, it seemed, grown up. She came from Tunbridge Wells, she said, and her name was Joan Wolfe.

During the conversation, the naïve, simplistic, honest Joan blurted out a great deal of her life story. She had come to Godalming looking for work and had stayed with an old lady at Thursley, a village about four miles away. She was engaged to a Canadian called Francis but they had been denied permission to marry as he was due to be shipped home. They walked in a local park where the little convent girl told the Canadian that her father had gassed himself and she did not get on with her mother. At this point, a patrolling policeman moved them on and they wandered up the hill, past the bridge towards Milford Crossroads, where Edwin Lutyens built his Red House overlooking the sleepy, meandering Wey. He kissed her. In the veiled legal language of the day: 'Did you ask her if she would go with you?' 'Yes.' 'Did you have connexion with her?' 'Yes. She did not want to for a while, but I persuaded her.' He left her in the roadway below the little Victorian railway station. She told him she had somewhere to stay in Godalming that night. It was half past eleven.

So the convent girl, so recently bereft of one sweetheart, had met another and within hours of their meeting had intercourse with him in a Surrey field, 'up a hill on the right-hand side of the road'. The hillside now bristles with large, burglar-alarmed houses. He arranged to see her the following night, Saturday, in the same pub. He tried again on the Sunday, but she didn't turn up.

He didn't see her again until the following Tuesday, between six and seven in the evening. Sangret and a comrade named Hartnell were standing outside a fish and chip shop. With the passage of time and the arrival of international fast-food chains, the humble fish and chip shop seems to have vanished from Godalming town centre. Joan joined them from the pictures – no longer in action, sad to say – and stood talking to them for about an hour and a half. It became clear that she had a date with Hartnell and he passed her a note. Joan read it and said, 'No.' Hartnell suggested that he tossed a coin to decide who would have her. Joan refused to play ball and Hartnell left.

Again the police arrived. It seemed that the whole relationship between these two was fated to be dogged by the police. They were there at its beginning and they presided in a way over its end. On that Tuesday, Constable Timothy Halloran – according to Greeno 'one of the gems; a man with his eyes open' – asked Joan to accompany him to the station and told Sangret he could come along too if he wanted to. They walked the length of the High Street in the blackout at nine forty-five, the constable with his measured tread of 2½ miles an hour, the Canadian soldier with his dark good looks and the thin-looking girl in her green and white dress. The station has gone now, nestling as it did between the British school built in 1812 and the river. A fire station stands on the site, seventy years on. Halloran believed that the girl would come under the Children and Young Persons Act as a likely runaway. Joan was whisked away into a side room to be quizzed by the constable. Halloran had turned up before Hartnell left. Perhaps the adjacency of an obvious runaway and the law unnerved the soldier. Joan's identity card had a Reading address and she told the constable she had no relatives and that her parents were dead. She had come to Godalming, she said, about three weeks before to be married to a Canadian soldier named Hearn. She'd picked the church – the Congregational – and the minister – the Reverend Newton Jones. Halloran rang the Reading police, who told him that Joan's address was Tunbridge Wells and that her mother was in fact still alive. When the constable confronted her with this, Joan said, 'To me my mother is dead.'

Sangret, in a different room, was asked for his pay book, which he produced. After half an hour, he took Joan back to Witley camp where he was stationed. Nothing of the Canadian camps on Witley Common remains. A National Trust centre lies to the north west of them, but all I could find of the 'parade ground' the warden described to me was an open stretch of spinney and bracken, a quiet oasis in the surrounding forest of conifers where ramblers and nature lovers wander today the criss-crossing paths with their red, blue and yellow markers.

The great artery of the A3 has so carved up this part of the Surrey countryside that it is difficult to imagine the leafy lanes as they once were, before the advent of street lights and double yellow lines and roaring traffic.

There are those who remember the camps well. A collection of timber and zinc buildings, dismantled at the end of the war, they were described by ex-Constable A.W. Bundy, who stood watch over Joan's body on the night she was found, as 'holding units'. Officially, they were designated Camps 101, 102 and 103. Sangret was stationed in 103, in Hut E2, and one of these, or perhaps all of them, are variously referred to as 'Jasper Camp' or 'Witley Camp'. Another one, on Thursley Common, Constable Bundy remembers as Tweedsmuir Camp or Number 1 NETD (Non-Effectives Transport Depot). It was manned by the Canadian Lorne Scots Regiment. Yet another seems to have been called Laurentide Camp.

Greeno, rushed into the area as an outsider, rather as we are today, describes them. There was a camp 'where illiterates from Canada's prairies and backwoods studied three months and then left'; a camp where Americans, 'switching from the Canadian Army to their own now that America was in the war, were sent for clearance – maybe for a couple of days or a couple of weeks and then moved on.' And there was, somewhere to the north-west of Thursley, 'the camp where British marines went to train and be hardened and then returned to their units.'

Here, in the undergrowth near Witley Camp, Joan and Sangret made love again – 'I had connexion with her that night and she did not object.' It was ten o'clock and Joan had no bed for the night. Behind the officers' quarters he made her 'a little shack with limbs and stuff' – the first of the 'wigwams' which gave Joan and her murder their bizarre nickname. He left her at six the following morning, arranging to meet that night at the fish and chip shop trysting place. Once again she stood him up.

Two days later, she wrote to him from the emergency ward in Warren Road Hospital, Guildford. It was Thursday 23 July – the Moon When Ducks Begin to Moult.

> 'My Dear August,
> 'Well, my dear, I hope I am forgiven for not turning up to see you last night, but I was in the police station five hours and they did not help me. I was walking along the road and suddenly came over queer. I fainted for the first time in my whole life. They brought me to the hospital

here. They are going to examine me. I shall know whether I am all right or not then. I hope you will come and see me, as I really want to see you very much and being in bed all day is awful. You can come any night between 6-7 p.m. and Sunday afternoon. Please try and come. I have your picture on the locker beside me. The nurses know you are my boyfriend, they told me to tell you to come and see me. You have to tell them my name and ask for Emergency Ward. Well, hoping to see you soon, I will say au revoir. God bless you. Love Joan.'

It was not strictly true that the police had not helped, although the advice they gave was probably not what Joan had wanted to hear. Constable Halloran tried to persuade her to go to the Church Army hostel at Guildford 'so she could be looked after, that is to say, she could ultimately go to work daily, and where she could sleep at night under some authority.' She told Halloran that she was in love with Sangret and they were trying to get married (this, the day after she had told the same constable that she had been due to marry Private Hearn). It seems likely that Joan's coming over 'queer' had taken place in Guildford itself.

Perhaps it was Sergeant Hicks of the Scottish Toronto Regiment, based in Camp 103, who read Sangret the letter, as it was Sergeant Hicks who wrote his reply. For August Sangret was a Métis, a '*bois brûlé*' or burnt wood, a Cree/French Indian, who could neither read nor write anything beyond his name.

Sangret went to visit Joan on the following Sunday, but he'd missed visiting hours and was turned away. She wrote to him again, more insistent, more explicit, that same night. And she had some news . . .

'Dear August,
'Well, I hope you are well as I have not seen or heard from you. Did you receive my last letter,

as I was not sure of the name of the camp? I wish with all my heart that I could see you, it is so very lonely here without anyone to speak to and there is so much I want to tell you. They are going to try and get me somewhere to stay in Godalming, or if this is not possible in Guildford. That will be nice because we will be able to see each other. Just one week has passed since I have known you, dear. It seems such a long time. I shall be in here about a fortnight and if you want to see me the visiting hours are 7-8 p.m. every night and Sunday afternoon 2-4 p.m. I hope you will try and come to see me, as I want to tell you when I can come out because someone will have to meet me and you are all I have in the world. Of course if you do not want to come I shall understand, August, but I am sure I shall never understand men. I do not know enough about them, but I can live and learn. Anyway I am pretty sure we are going to have a tiny wee one, maybe that is why you do not want to come and see me because you think that. I hope not anyway, but dear, I would not blame you one little bit, if you did not want to marry me because I really am too young and too old-fashioned to be married. I regret what we did now it is too late, for I still say it is wicked. I hope God forgives me, for I am truly sorry, and do not want to do anything wrong really, I guess you think I am silly, and I suppose I am, but remember I was brought up in a very strict Catholic school for 13½ years, that is why I am so old-fashioned. We were taught that to have a baby before you was married was a sin. I cannot yet believe it of me, what would my Priest at home say, and my people would not have anything to do with me. Oh dear, August, why did we do it, you will not want to marry me anyway, because we hardly know one another, and I do not know anything about babies . . . Well, I suppose I shall have to close this letter now, if I want to get it posted, so au revoir (daddy). God bless you always dear, Joan.'

He had given her his address that night as they lay under the Surrey stars, wrapped in the sweet-smelling pine of the wigwam he'd made her. He had given her his photograph. They had discussed marriage. What he had not given her, at least by a careful reckoning of the dates, was his baby. If the pregnancy was anything but a part of a lonely girl's fertile imagination, it was not a pregnancy brought about by August Sangret. His supposed subsequent actions were therefore all the more unnecessary. In the letter that Sergeant Hicks wrote in reply, Sangret said he was quite prepared to marry the girl – he said the same thing to his defence counsel, Linton Thorp, at his trial.

Joan came to see him at the camp on her release from hospital, on the following Tuesday. She missed him then, but caught up with him while he was attending a class. She passed him a note, which of course he couldn't read and which the ever-indulgent Sergeant Hicks may have read to him, and he found her skulking in the trees between Camps 102 and 103. She told him that she had sent two boys with a message for him the night before, but they had told Joan he was away on manoeuvres. Who told them that is unknown, but in any case it was untrue and the lovers had missed each other. They spoke of marriage and she told him that she was 'in trouble'.

'By that,' asked Linton Thorp at the trial, 'you understand that she was in the family way?'

'Yes,' Sangret answered.

For about an hour they talked, and they arranged to meet that evening in Godalming. They walked around the town for a while and he brought her back to the makeshift shack behind the officers' lines, where he added more branches to the wigwam. It was Thursday, 30 July. He answered roll call, then doubled back with two blankets from Hut E2 and spent the night with her. During the night, for whatever reason, he rummaged through Joan's handbag and found the trinkets later spilled in Houndown Wood – the Bible and the crucifix. There were photographs of her dead father, of Sangret himself and of other soldiers. He gave her two ten shilling notes and noticed (for the first time?) a wedding ring on her left hand, given to her by 'her boyfriend' Francis.

At the end of July, as it now was, Joan was working in the canteen of a balloon factory somewhere near Godalming. The 31st may have been her first day there. The making of barrage balloons to thwart enemy aircraft had become a major industry by 1942. Barrage balloons formed an aerial canopy over any area which might be a target for attacking aircraft. Such raids were not as likely by '42 as they had been earlier, but the balloons stayed nonetheless. They were usually sausage-shaped, made of cotton or rubber, 63 feet long and with a capacity of 19,150 cubic feet. Each had three fins which kept it balanced and its nose to the wind. The balloons floated at a maximum height of 6,000 feet and were attached to the ground by steel cables fitted to a mobile winch. The object was to make German aircraft fly high enough to avoid them and so make them more vulnerable to fighter attack by the RAF.

Joan was paid £2 10s a week. Life in the wigwam went on for a week or so, always following the same pattern. She would go to work, or so he believed. He would go to classes, to improve his non-existent formal education. He would carry out manoeuvres at the camp. Then he would answer roll call and abscond, slipping through the birches and the pines to their ramshackle home. As always, Greeno put a less rosy gloss on it: 'She allowed herself to be ordered about like a dog, to be left shut in a shack all day till her master returned at night.'

At some time early in August, Joan met Sangret in Godalming and told him she had lost her job because of bad timekeeping. Sangret gave her money and suggested she find somewhere else to live. Joan told him she wanted to go home, but could not until she received a reply to the letter she had written to her mother. No reply came. She went away for three days to London and Sangret did not hear from her.

When she came back, Sangret got meat and fruit pies and cakes from the camp canteen and they sat together in the wigwam, eating them. Private Donald Brett, of the Cape Breton Highlanders, attached to the Military Police at Jasper Camp, found them and moved them on. The girl was on army property and had no right to be there.

Brett, with power to arrest soldiers breaking regulations, continued on his patrol. When he returned that way twenty minutes later, the pair had gone, but an army kitbag and a large pack were left behind. The kitbag contained a lady's purse, army clothing and coupons, together with Joan's identity card. At nine that night, Brett saw Sangret again, and shone his torch in his face. He gave him the choice of opening the kitbag he had just lifted from the wigwam there or in the guard house. Sangret complied grudgingly and then returned to his quarters.

On the Sunday, Joan was taken away temporarily (by the police, who returned her to hospital in Guildford), but could find no other accommodation in the area and drifted back. This time Sangret built another shack, behind the sergeants' lines, the branches cut with his army issue, tin-handled jack-knife and made waterproof with his rain cape and his gas cape. The next morning, he got some bread from a house nearby and planned to walk into Witley to find a room for Joan. In the event they didn't get there.

There is some confusion over dates during this period. Joan was in hospital, according to the matron at Warren Road, from 23 August (a Sunday) to 1 September. 30 July was the first time the couple slept together in the first wigwam, which leaves nearly three weeks unaccounted for. Sangret told the judge at his trial that they slept in the shack behind the officers' lines for two weeks until Brett found them and in the later one, behind the sergeants' lines, for two nights. They spent the Sunday looking for rooms. They bought some bread at a tea-shop and Sangret noticed the red-capped Military Police searching for them. Joan had gone on ahead. When he found she wasn't at the new wigwam, he went to the guard room at Witley Camp. She was there, 'with the Provost Men'.

Joan went back into hospital that evening, taken there by the Surrey police. At eleven in the morning, Sangret was arrested by the MPs. The charge was keeping a girl in camp and he was allowed to talk to her before the pair were separated. They also spoke to a civilian policeman and Joan told him of the couple's plans to marry.

On 24 August, Sangret received a letter from Joan, from the Warren Road Hospital in Guildford.

> 'My Darling,
> 'Well, you can see by my address that I am in hospital again, not anything particular this time, but because I have got nowhere to stay. They are going to keep me here until we get married and then they will fix something up for me. They will look after me properly and I have a bath every day and clean clothes, while the other ones are washed, and now it will give me a chance to get my own clothes sent here. I am writing to my mother again too. I will be all dressed up to get married then. I am asking my mother to come and see me because the [police] officer told me I have to get her consent to get married. I know she will give it to me. Gosh, darling, they all treat me as if I was ill here, just because of the baby; I mustn't do this or that. I told them I have never let it bother me, and they were horrified when they heard how we had been living, just as if that makes any difference. Gosh, I was never ill when you looked after me, I was happy anyway. I will never regret what we have done, we had had some good laughs, and tears too. (Oh! Burning wood, the loveliest smell in the world). I will

never forget that, will you? Those old ladies must have wondered what we started laughing at. I missed you very much, my darling, last night, it was ever so lonely. I am so used to talking to you, and then listening to you, groaning to yourself because I would not let you sleep. When I turned over, I missed you putting your arms round me, I never thought it would be so lonely. I did not sleep much, I was thinking about you being shut up in the Guard House, and if you missed me too, and hoping and praying that you will not get into too much trouble, because if it had not been for me, you would never have slept out or taken military property. I should be the one to get into trouble, not you, and they did not say anything to me. It is not fair that you should get into a row, but I have faith in God, and am praying every day for Him to look after you and me and see that you do not get into too much trouble. I am sure that whatever happens it will be for the best, because He knows how much we love one another, and anyway it will help us to be married sooner. If you have asked the Officer tell me all he has to say when you write and let me know how things are going. If you have not got enough money to write to me, ask one of the MPs to post it for you. I am sure they will, because I want to know what is happening, an if you can get permission to be married. So write back as soon as you get this letter, please, Sweetheart. It is certainly going to be very lonely without anyone. We have always been together until now. The old fire in the evenings and the blackberries and heaps of little things we used to do. The guards that watched us through their field glasses as we walked across

the fields through the heather. We have so
many things to talk about and to laugh at. Well,
it is going to rain today, I am sure. I hope our
home keeps dry even though we are not there.
In this ward there are six beds, and all of them
are empty except the one I am in, and so you
can guess how lonely it is, but I can console
myself by writing to you. You know I am in a
safe place now anyway, and you will not be able
to accuse me of going out with other soldiers. I
have never done it since I have known you
anyway, but you are so damned jealous you
think it; but still we will forget all that now and
look forward to the future, when we are
married. I know we will be happy even if you
are a horrible Canadian. I guess I must say
Good night, my Darling, and God bless you.
Don't forget whatever happens I will always
love you and always be true to you, and every
night I will be thinking of you. I will write again
soon, Darling, and keep smiling, for soon we
will be together for always, and if you cannot
get permission to marry me now I will wait for
you until after the war and then we will be. But
I hope we will be married very soon because of
the baby, and because I love you more than
anything else in the world. Joan.'

Under escort on the following morning, Monday 24 August,
Sangret was taken to his commanding officer, Major Talmadge
Ross Gray, and asked his permission to marry Joan. Gray
pointed out what the policeman had to Joan – that she needed
her mother's permission 'because she was still technically a
minor' and official permission for Sangret had to be obtained
from the Canadian government. Gray then released Sangret to
find the girl and gave him £1 to do so. He discovered she was
at the hospital when her letter arrived – 'I got someone to read

it to me' – and asked someone to phone on his behalf. He visited her at Guildford on Saturday, 29 August, 'around 2 o'clock'. They discussed the marriage plans and Sangret slipped Joan the ten shillings he still had left from Gray's pound. During the following week, Sangret visited Gray again, this time to retrieve the written note found later among the leaf mould near Joan's body. On the next Sunday, 30 August, Sangret obtained a pass to visit Joan again. They talked. She told him face to face how lonely she was and that she would like her freedom 'because she was not sick or anything. But she agreed to stay where she was until the wedding or until they found somewhere more suitable. He next saw her on Tuesday, 1 September. This time, she had obtained a pass from the matron and had come to see him.

Assistant Matron Margaret Strong recognized Joan from the photograph shown at the trial. On 1 September, she had signed Joan's pass and given her clothes to go out, among them the green and white dress in which she died. Either Joan had lied to the matron about her motives or she had decided on an impulse to keep on going once she was out and to find Sangret. It was an impulse that led to her death. She mentioned going shopping, then to the pictures. There was no mention of her boyfriend. She was due back at five o'clock. Margaret Strong never saw her again.

They walked towards Godalming, made somewhere on the way – 'she was quite willing' – and had tea at the NAAFI building in the town. He saw her off from the station at half-past nine.

The next day was a route march. Sangret's unit, with rifles and full pack, were marching over the common, preparing for whatever the mysterious big push was that had been planned somewhere in the corridors of power. Between one and two o'clock, he saw a girl with scrubbed face, smiling with her buck teeth, the sun glinting on the crucifix round her neck. She sat by the roadside, her knees hunched up under her chin, her arms hugging her ankles. He waved to her. By half past four, the march was over and Sangret was dismissed. Joan was still there. She told Sangret she had got a pass and was afraid to go back as it was so late. She had spent the previous night at the railway station.

They decided the best plan would be for her to stay at Miss Hayter's house in Thursley. Thor's Lee is a slightly odd name for a village miles to the south west of the edge of the Danelaw. It straddles the old A3, the London-Portsmouth road, where according to a gravestone in Thursley churchyard, a sailor was done to death by three travellers in 1768. Violent death, it seems, is no stranger to this quiet part of Surrey.

The old Half Moon has gone now; so has the Red Lion. Of the three original village pubs, redolent of the great coaching days that spanned the late eighteenth and early nineteenth centuries, only the Three Horse Shoes remains. Ironically, it is not mentioned in any literature of the wigwam Murder. The Half Moon, by Hammer Pond, seems to have been demolished to make the new A3(M), altering for ever the lie of the land.

Kate Hayter, referred to by Sangret as the 'old lady', lived at The Bungalow in Kettlebury, half a mile or so outside the village of Thursley itself. Joan had stayed with her on the night of 15 July the day before Francis Hearn left her. Sangret returned to camp, told Provost-Sergeant Harold Wade that Joan was back and got some tea and a water-bottle from the canteen for her. By the time he rejoined Joan she was already talking to a 'soldier boy' Sangret knew by sight, but not by name.

Together they looked for Miss Hayter's house, but in the dark it took them some time and when they got there, the 'old lady' appeared to be in bed. Not wishing to wake her and afraid of her spaniel – 'the dog always barks and he might bite' – Joan spent the night with Sangret in Thursley cricket pavilion. The present pavilion is not the one what became a makeshift home for the lovers. It was demolished after the war, but a local man who has been kind enough to help me with this book still has the weathered boards with the strange, sad poetry of Joan Wolfe. This was 3 September, the third anniversary of the outbreak of war. Sangret collected his water-bottle, a blanket, answered roll call and repeated the forty-five-minute walk back to the pavilion again the following night. This pattern continued until 9 September, Sangret bringing the basics of an evening meal for them both from the NAAFI. Joan told Sangret that there was no room at Miss Hayter's because her sister was staying, but there would be as soon as the sister left.

William Featherby was a jobbing builder who lived at The Bungalow, Thursley (a house I was unable to identify on my visits there). More pertinently to the peculiarities of wartime, he was head Air Raid Precaution warden for the area. There had been a second pavilion on the edge of the cricket green and it had burnt down; the heat had scorched the planking of the one left standing. Fire is always a hazard in a country area so heavily wooded and the target it presented for enemy bombers didn't bear thinking about. Accordingly, Warden Featherby was doubly alert.

On the 7th or 8th, at about four in the afternoon, he saw Joan, whom he recognized from the day before when he had seen her picking blackberries at the edge of the common, cooking vegetables over an open fire. She was still there at seven that evening, even though Featherby had told her she should not be there. (It says much for the parochialness of pre-war England that no one mentions the pavilion doors being locked, or Sangret or Joan breaking and entering – the modern pavilion, but contrast, is heavily padlocked).

Sangret was inside the building by the time of Featherby's second visit. The warden told them both that it was against the law to light a fire under the terms of the Property Act and the penalty was £5. He let them stay there that night, but warned them that he would be forced to call the police is they were still there the next day. The threat seems to have worked, as neither of them was there after the 9th – according to him, anyway.

The last time Sangret said he saw Joan was on the morning of Monday 14th. He had gone back to the camp and she was going back to the old lady's, to see if her sister had left.

And no one, apart from her murderer, saw her again. The love affair of Joan Pearl Wolfe and August Sangret had lasted for eighty-one days.

5

Softly, Softly . . .

Monday, 14 September was pay day. Joseph Wells of the Regina Rifle Regiment stood in line for two hours before he got his and that night decided to spend some of it at the Half Moon pub in Thursley. On the way he met August Sangret, the Métis he had known as a kid back home in Battleford. He was on his way to meet his girl, Joan. Wells, who may have been a Métis too, had met the girl once. She had been knitting, he remembered. But that night Joan wasn't around. The Half Moon was crowded out with Canadians drinking their pay so the soldiers went on to the Red Lion or the Three Horse Shoes and Wells got the drinks while Sangret walked over to the pavilion. In fifteen minutes, he was back. Joan hadn't turned up.

'She must be mad at me,' Sangret told Wells, 'because I did not come early enough.' Twice while Wells was in the pub, he had gone out to look for her, the second time not returning for half an hour. She was not at the pavilion. When they got there it was already dusk and Sangret called her name two or three times. Her knitting was still there and a groundsheet wedged into a bush, but of Joan there was no sign. Wells told Sangret that he was crazy, that no girl would stay alone in the dark at that time of night. Sangret told him he didn't know Joan. They heard a dog barking nearby and Sangret told Wells that must be Joan going to knock up the old lady for the night. Perhaps his Indian blood gave him the direction. How else would he know the dog was Kate Hayter's spaniel? Unless it was wishful thinking. Unless ...

They rummaged around and called her name for nearly an hour. Sangret found her stockings and his blanket as well as some bags they had stolen. Assuming that Joan was now tucked up at Miss Hayter's, the two made their way back to camp. Sangret told Private Patrick Anderson, in the next bed to his, that he couldn't find Joan – she must have gone home.

Wells' account of that Monday evening does not exactly tally with Sangret's in terms of precise times and where they drank, but there is no major discrepancy.

On the following day, Sangret returned to Miss Hayter's, still in search of Joan. Kate Hayter's evidence on this at the trial is rather vague. She said she had first met Sangret on the morning of 15 July, the night Joan had first stayed with her. Joan, however, was already a regular fixture by this time as she walked past The Bungalow every day with the soldier Kate Hayter calls her husband, a man she knew later as Francis, and another one called 'Pop'. After 16 July, she never saw Joan again. She claimed to have seen Sangret next 'five or six weeks later' (which would be in the middle of August) and he asked if Joan was there. She was not. 'About a fortnight or three weeks afterwards' (which was probably Tuesday 15 September, although she remembered the day as a Sunday) he arrived again, asking the same question. According to Sangret, the 'old lady' 'was not in very good humour, I guess and she said "No" and closed the door.'

Miss Hayter remembered Sangret being more voluble, talking about marrying Joan, saying he was very fond of her, that she had promised to meet him the day before and that she had not turned up. Curiously, under cross-examination by Sangret's counsel, she denied having seen the Canadian until he turned up at her side door looking for Joan on the first occasion. Minutes earlier she had told Mr Geoffrey Lawrence, for the Crown, that she had met him on 15 July. She did remember however that on Sangret's second – or was it the third – visit (15 September) 'he seemed very much upset . . . he looked very sad'. She pointed out to him that Joan was already married to the Canadian soldier, Francis, but Sangret assured her this was not the case. It is a pity that no record now exists of the closing speeches for the prosecution or defence in this case, because Miss Hayter seems a very shaky witness. Not only do her dates not accord as to when Sangret came in search of Joan, she also has him turning up only two days after he was transferred to the area and, according to her, Sangret came with Joan to her bungalow two days before the pair actually met!

On Saturday the 19th, Sangret went to Godalming to widen his search. It was the opinion of his bunk-mate, Anderson, and Miss Hayter that Joan must have gone home, but that seemed to make no sense. As far as Joan was concerned, she had no home to go to. In the park where he and Joan had walked – an eternity before – on the night they had first met, Sangret met a local or a soldier named Ennear, sitting on a seat. He hadn't seen Joan, but would keep his eyes open. On Monday, in desperation, he went to see Provost-Sergeant Wade.

The Provost's department in the army is in charge of discipline. The Provost-Marshal, working out of Headquarters staff under the Adjutant-General, is responsible for maintaining order, arresting offenders who have broken regulations and catching deserters. Such an officer is attached to each army corps in wartime and under him a unit of military policemen or Provost's men see to the daily running of their particular camps.

Harold Redvers Wade, of the Canadian Grenadier Guards, was head of the MPs at Jasper Camp, Witley. He had been involved with Sangret and his girl since late August when he had arrested Sangret for having a girl on army property. He discovered Joan's name and even visited her at Warren Road Hospital, Guildford. Wade seems to have been the avuncular type who felt sorry for the pair and was all set to get a subscription going. Joan's absconding from hospital made him think twice however, and the last time he saw her was on 8

September. She was walking with Sangret on the road near Thursley.

Wade's memory of Sangret's visit to him on Monday the 21st was fuller than the private's and had a bearing on later events that turned out to sound sinister in court. With the instincts of a policemen, Wade asked Sangret what he thought had made Joan vanish. The private shrugged. He did not know, but eventually admitted that they had quarrelled, he having told her he didn't care whether they married or not. So why make a fuss, Wade asked, if he didn't intend to marry her? Sangret told him that 'if she was found and anything had happened to her, he did not want to be mixed up in it.' Sangret did not give Wade the address of Miss Hayter; nor did he show him where her house was.

Sangret's testimony at his trial was that he asked Wade if he had heard from Joan's mother. Wade had no recollection of this. It was difficult to gauge Sangret's reaction to Joan's disappearance because 'he is the type of man with what we call a poker face, and it is hard to say just what is going on in his mind.' Wade's problem was that he should not have become so involved with the pair. Technically, Sangret was under his jurisdiction, as far as discipline was concerned, while he was attached to the camp attending classes under the auspices of the Educational Company. Sangret had reported Joan missing on the Wednesday or Thursday after her disappearance (i.e. 16 or 17 September) and by the 21st, it seemed to Wade as though whatever fondness Sangret had once felt for Joan had changed into an uncaring attitude. Sangret lied to Wade on this occasion, telling him that Joan had been staying at the 'old lady's'. He did this, he said, to avoid confessing that they had been together, either at the wigwams or the cricket pavilion.

For the next two and a half weeks all was quiet on the home front. At some point during this time, the prosecution was later to allege, August Sangret returned to the hollow where he had roughly buried Joan Wolfe and dragged her corpse to higher ground. Why he did this was never ascertained, but he piled earth on her body, not noticing the scratches on her legs or the hank of hair which detached itself from her shattered and bloody scalp. Not dreaming that a tracked vehicle would dislodge the grave. Not dreaming that a watchful Marine would spot his victim's rat-gnawed finger, pointing accusingly from the earth, towards Kettlebury, where the 'old lady' lived.

And the war went on. While Sangret went to his classes and tramped Hankley Common on his route marches, the British Army invaded Madagascar and the Eighth Army carried out a series of lightning raids near the village of El Alamein. On the Eastern Front, Hitler's Panzers came to the bloody full stop that was Stalingrad.

September turned into October. The Snow Goose began to fly south.

On a hilltop in Houndown Wood, the blow-fly eggs developed into maggots and began to feed on Joan Pearl Wolfe.

Then they found the body.

The love affair, if that is what it was, between Sangret and Joan Wolfe had been extraordinarily public. There were many reasons for this. Even in wartime, a teenaged girl, living rough and a long way from home, was likely to be noticed. For all Macdonald Critchley refers to girls in the plural hanging around the Witley camps, I have come across specific evidence of no others. And the hysteria of a nation at war increased the number of 'little Hitlers', in uniform and out of it, who snooped and gossiped and moved people on. In the little pond that was rural Surrey, the police seem to have been especially vigilant. Their task was made countless times more difficult by the presence of soldiers, and foreigners at that, with their own internal discipline and their own code of behaviour. There again, Sangret's illiteracy meant that he was unable to cope with Joan's schoolgirlish letters. Their romance could never be private, because he needed a go-between, an interpreter. For such a man to embark on murder at such a time was folly in the extreme. When Joan's body was found, her rat-gnawed finger could only be pointing at him. As Eric Neve for the Prosecution was to say at Sangret's trial, 'Who else but August?' And for all Greeno claims to have interviewed thousands of people in the space of two months, my belief is that his focus shifted hardly at all from August Sangret.

Let us look again at the Surrey constabulary's involvement with Joan. Constable Timothy Halloran had been patrolling his monotonous 2½ mph beat along the High Street in Godalming for some time. It was nine forty-five. A warm night. 21 July. He saw a young, scruffy girl in the company of two soldiers. Modern readers will not appreciate the role of the police in the '40s. Halloran and his superior Superintendent Webb were probably coppers of the old school. Catch a kid scrumping apples and you clip him round the ear and take him home to his dad, who will almost certainly belt him again. Catch a girl loitering on street corners with soldiers . . . well, you know what they're after. Take her aside, ask some questions, give her a fatherly chat, try to get her out of harm's way.

The girl wore a crucifix around her neck. Her identity card bore a Reading address. The girl had no home and no relatives, she told Halloran. Her parents were dead. She had come to Godalming three weeks earlier to be married to a Canadian soldier named Hearn. The vicar was the Reverend Newton Jones of the Congregational church. Halloran didn't like the look of her rough clothes, her matted hair, her unwashed face. He took her to the station and checked her identity card. The soldier came with her.

She was back the next day, as instructed, and she was wearing a rosary. Then she stayed in the Church Army hostel in Guildford which the police had arranged for her. About a week later, Halloran saw her in the High Street, wearing the green and white dress in which she died. By this time, Joan had the job at the balloon factory.

Joan had lied to the police and Halloran knew she had. Reading police told him over the phone that the girl's address was Tunbridge Wells and that her mother was still alive. 'To me,' she had told him, 'my mother is dead.' She also told the constable that she was in love with Sangret and they were trying to get married. Although Halloran did not speak to the soldier, nor Sangret to him, the couple seemed genuinely fond of each other.

Halloran was also present on 23 August when she was brought again into the station. This time, however, the matter was more serious and it was Superintendent Richard Webb of the Surrey CID who handled things. It was this chance meeting which enabled the detective to identify the body of Joan Wolfe so quickly. Webb had seen Joan briefly when Halloran brought her in the first time, and agreed at the trial that she was in need of protection and 'was rather dirty on that occasion'. Now he had the chance of a long chat with the girl and he took it. She was, in the modern parlance of the social services, 'at risk'. She was leading an immoral life, but Webb would not, at the trial, be drawn on this. She was not a prostitute, because although she lived rough and her lifestyle had much to be desired, she was utterly loyal to one soldier at a time. Like Halloran, Webb believed that she intended to marry Sangret. He remembered her as being a well-spoken, quiet girl, very healthy-looking.

In the rather naïve and moralistic way of the time, the elderly Mr Justice Macnaghten at Sangret's trial asked, 'Did she look like a prostitute?'

'No, she was a very well-spoken and a very quiet-spoken girl.'

'She did not look a bad girl?'

'No,' answered Webb. 'When you spoke to her you got the impression that she was a good-living girl by the way she spoke. She had a very charming way with her.'

It cannot happen often that a policeman gets a chance to talk, not only to a victim whose murder he subsequently investigates, but to the victim's alleged killer too. But it was so with Webb. On 24 August, Sangret turned up at Godalming police station looking for Joan. Webb told him told him that she had been sent to the Warren Road Institution at Guildford. He said to the soldier, 'Joan tells me she is pregnant and you are responsible.' 'Yes,' said Sangret and asked if he could visit Joan in hospital. Webb explained that that was up to the matron. 'We have been living together in a shack,' the soldier went on. 'I am fond of her and want to marry her.'

Webb advised that Joan be allowed to stay where she was until the marriage could be arranged. The next time he saw Joan, her rotting, partially mummified body was protruding from the mound in Houndown Wood. The next time he saw Sangret, he charged him with her murder.

Nor was it only the police who witnessed their love affair. On 10 September, four children – twelve-year-old Rita Bonner and her brother Derek, together with their friends Grace White and Audrey Saint – saw Joan and Sangret attempt to find rooms for the girl in Witley. Sangret was picking blackberries and seemed relatively unconcerned when no rooms appeared to be available. He told Rita he was going back to camp. Grace remembered harsh words between the lovers. 'You will not help me find any rooms,' Joan had snapped. 'You will only stand about.' Interestingly, however, there was no reaction from Sangret, no flare of temper, no sign of fight. A week or so later, Rita saw Sangret again, on his own this time in Cramhurst Lane, Witley (misspelt as Bramhurst in the trial testimony), which runs parallel with Yew Tree Lane, where the Bonners lived at number 1. He was looking for Joan and told the little girl that they had found rooms at the White Lion in Milford. The pub still offers 'guest beers' but no guest rooms. The A3 thunders past its front doors and its peeling paint sign. It is difficult to imagine the little Victorian building as it must have been in the quieter, slower days of the '40s. Derek had just started work as a gardener's boy. Fifty years on, he still remembered Sangret's quietness and he had in his possession the Canadian's cap badge as a souvenir of those days. Rita remembered it as if it were yesterday; their mother did not like the idea of a stranger (Joan) staying in their house – it was wartime and you couldn't be too careful. The pair were very quiet; Joan was scruffy and very thin, wearing a headscarf. Audrey still has a photograph of the old Witley Camp, now long demolished.

Alice Curtis of Brook, to the south-east of Witley Park, saw the couple on Friday, 11 September on Witley Common. She was on the bus to Godalming and was passing Gasden Lane which would upward to the camps. She recognized at the trial the tin can that Joan had been carrying, the one she used to collect blackberries. She saw them again on the following day and on the Sunday, walking on both occasions towards Brook at midday. She recognized Joan by her photograph and remembered the green and white dress. Oddly, she could not swear to the man being Sangret. He was dark and had black hair, but that was as far as she was prepared to go.

Arthur Robinson was a roadman working for the council, living at Yew Tree Cottage, Thursley (which I was unable to locate during my visits there). He was repairing the road on Dye House Hill opposite the cricket pavilion early in September and on the 7th or 8th saw Joan sitting outside it as though she had just woken up, wrapped in a dark blanket. The next morning he saw her again, combing her hair and on the following day, blackberrying with a tin can.

We have already noted ARP Warden William Featherby's observations of the pair living in the pavilion.

What did Sangret's comrades in arms make of the liaison? Charles Hicks was a sergeant with the Toronto Scottish Regiment of Canada. On 6 July he was posted to Witley, Camp 103, to act as instructor. At the end of July, Sangret asked him to read a letter he had just received from Joan, then in the Warren Road Hospital. They discussed the likelihood of Sangret's being the father of Joan's child after a mere two weeks and Hicks' advice was that Sangret ought to sort it out quickly. During this conversation, Sangret said he was in love with Joan and asked Hicks the procedure for marriage. Hicks saw them together in the first week of August on the road to Godalming. On 15 September, Sangret asked Hicks' permission to skip a class to go blackberrying. On the understanding that these were for the Sergeants' Mess, Hicks agreed. Having had no luck at selling the berries at the Mess (he usually got 7 shillings) Sangret eventually sold them to Hicks for 4 shillings. In *War on the Underworld*, Ted Greeno proffers a sinister – and ludicrous – ulterior motive for this blackberrying jaunt. On 27 September, Hicks asked Sangret how his 'little affair' was getting on. He was astounded to be told that the girl had disappeared. 'Are you kidding?' he asked. The poker-faced Sangret had replied, 'No.' Hicks asked if he had made an attempt to contact her. Sangret had told him that he had had a letter written, but it had come back with 'Unknown Here' written on the envelope. Hicks had seen this envelope himself. Sangret had not seemed unduly perturbed, but told Hicks that the Provost-Sergeant was helping to trace her.

Patrick Anderson served as a private in the Royal Canadian Engineers and shared a dormitory with Sangret in Hut E2 at Camp 103, Witley. It is from him that the court later learned of the Métis' nocturnal habits, his answering the roll call then disappearing to sleep with Joan beyond the officers' lines. Anderson had seen the couple together between Godalming and Witley and Sangret had told him bunk-mate that they intended to marry. It was to Anderson he confided that Joan was missing. She had gone away on a 'scheme' (Canadian army slang for manoeuvres) and the wedding was off 'because we chewed the fat last night', implying a quarrel. He didn't say what the row was about. Anderson assumed that Joan had gone home, but remembered Sangret 'seemed to be worried about something – I do not know what he was worried about. He seemed kind of restless.'

Just as the civilian police knew of the dangerous liaison, so the MPs of the Canadian Army kept a watchful eye on it. We have already heard the essence of Donald Brett's testimony. Lance-Corporal Alexander Shearer, of the Cape Breton Highlanders attached to the regiment, was patrolling the woods on 20 August when he and a comrade, Lance-Corporal

Naugler, came across a brush shack inhabited by a girl he later saw brought into the guard room by other MPs.

By 23 August, the army authorities could turn blind eyes to Sangret's behaviour no longer. Sergeant Harold Wade of the Canadian Grenadier Guards became involved at this stage as Sangret had been arrested for being found with the girl within the camp precincts.

Clarence Bear was a sapper in the Royal Canadian Engineers. He wrote two letters for Sangret. The first was to Joan in 'some hospital in Guildford' explaining that he had some money to give her and that Major Gray of the Education Company was arranging the marriage lines. More ominously, the second letter he wrote was a love letter to a woman in Glasgow – probably the mysterious Mrs Mary Pattigan – with whom Sangret wanted to spend fourteen days' leave. 'What will Miss Wolfe say if she finds out you are writing to this woman?' Bear asked. 'She will never find out,' Sangret told him. 'She has gone on a three weeks' course.'

Sangret made no secret of the fact that there were other women in his life. He was good looking and it is certain that women found him attractive. At his first hearing at Godalming, Greeno noticed a girl slipping sweets to Sangret. One sexual conquest was Mrs Leona Predeau who wrote to him from back home in Maidstone, Saskatchewan. She had left her husband and Sangret 'used to go with her. I used to have connexions with her.' Mrs Oak, of 21, Vesty Street, Halifax, Nova Scotia, seems to have been nothing more than a friend. Sangret probably met her when he was stationed in Halifax. She wrote to him every week but the letters began to dry up by September. Mr Oak was on the scene and Sangret seems to have been friendly with them both. She sent the soldier three parcels in the summer of 1942. The first contained fudge; the second, razor blades (Sangret used a safety razor – a Gillette army pattern – and Canadian blades), perfume (aftershave) and shaving cream; the third, candy. To the Military Police, Sangret said that these were 'girls', implying that they were at least potential lovers, and this explained the cooling of his passion for Joan by mid-October. Mary Pattigan, of 56, Greenfield Street, Glasgow, was a widow whose husband had been killed in the evacuation from Dunkirk. On leave in May, Sangret had met her at 'an amusement place' in Glasgow. She too wrote to him, but a letter he had had written for him, sent to her in late September, had been returned. He had not stayed with her.

If August Sangret intended to keep the affair with the prominent runaway under wraps, he had made a peculiarly bad job of it. Military policemen, civilian policemen, local adults, local children, army comrades – dozens of people knew all about Joan and her soldier. But to Chief Inspector Edward Greeno fell the task of finding Joan's murderer – and the mere existence of a lover was a world away from that.

The protocol of all this was tricky. This was the heyday of the trilby-hatted, pipe-smoking, lantern-jawed hero of detective fiction, but 'calling in the Yard' with its surrounding mystique often raised a wall of non-co-operation from the local force. In his autobiography, *Friends and Villains*, the late Tom Roberts, Head of Surrey CID, whom Keith Simpson describes as a 'quiet, most patient detective of long experience', remembered Superintendent Webb ringing him at about half-past six on the evening the body was found. When he joined the knot of men on the hillside, it was damp and misty – 'one of those misty, damping nights,' ex-Constable Bundy told me, 'which soak everything.'

When the immediate exhumation had taken place and Simpson and Gardner had come to their first conclusions, Roberts was summoned to the office of Major Nicholson, Surrey's Chief Constable. He told him that the victim, as yet, of course, unnamed, was likely to be one of the 'camp followers' who had drifted to the area, mostly from London, and who had already accounted for a pile of allegations and complaints on the plates of various Surrey desk sergeants.

If the dead girl came from London, then the Metropolitan Police were more than equipped to handle the enquiry, because they had the experience of such researches as a result of the blitz and evacuation. This would be all the more useful as the

Surrey force were stretched on wartime security work. Nicholson sanctioned it and Roberts range Superintendent Worth, in temporary charge of the CID at Scotland Yard. He promised Detective Chief Inspector Greeno and Detective Sergeant Hodge and that they would be in Roberts' office at Guildford within the hour. They were.

On 12 October, five days after Joan's decomposing body was found on Hankley Common, Greeno, his number two, Detective Sergeant Fred Hodge and Superintendent Webb went to Jasper Camp to interview August Sangret in Major Gray's office.

From *War on the Underworld*, it is clear that Greeno was not ready to tackle Sangret as early as this. He had only been in the area for four days. His reasoning for doing so however is odd. Sangret was due for leave which he intended to take, as he had in May, in Glasgow. Greeno was afraid that he'd lose his man if he didn't see him before that. In reality of course, having failed to find anything incriminating on 12 October, Greeno took a far greater risk. If Sangret was his man, he'd now be rattled, suspicious of the police. He'd be infinitely more likely to vanish somewhere on the road to Glasgow.

Corporal Robert Talbot of the Cape Breton Highlanders was on duty that morning when Sangret came in. Corporal Theodore Stiles of the same regiment was there too. Sangret told him that he had not seen Joan for over four weeks. He had been to the 'old lady's' at Thursley, but she hadn't been there. More ominously, he said, 'The last time I saw her we had a row over not getting married,' and 'I have a girl up in Scotland and one in Canada; I don't feel like getting married in this country.' Sangret seemed rather nervous when told that Sergeant Wade wanted to see him. Had he, perhaps, seen Webb's police car outside?

Greeno was careful, slow. For all Miss Lefebure likened him to a battleship, this was no time for a broadside. The old saying 'Softly, softly, catchee monkey' was tried and tested. With permission from the army, Greeno was able to take the Canadian to Godalming police station.

'I believe you have for some time been associating with a young woman named Joan Pearl Wolfe, aged nineteen years,' the Chief Inspector said. 'I should like you, if you will, to tell me all about your association with her, and what you know about her.'

Sangret's casual, 'Yes, all right,' resulted in one of the longest verbal statements ever made in a murder enquiry. It took five days to complete, ran to over 17,000 words – 58 pages – and every single one of them was written down by Sergeant Hodge. It featured as Exhibit 39 in Sangret's trial in December and occupied most of the first day's proceedings. It was so long that Eric Neve KC, for the Crown, lost his voice while reading it and Linton Thorp, for the defence, had to take over to finish it.

Sangret's leave began on the following Monday, five days away. Greeno recalled:

> 'While the man was paraded for pay I waited in the major's office with Sergeant Hodge and the local Superintendent, Webb. Nobody else knew why we were there except the provost sergeant, a wily old warrior named Wade who had been in the Coldstreams in World War One and who figured that Scotland Yard would not be there unless something serious was about.'

One of Wade's men had called Sangret back: 'Hey, soldier, you're wanted in the guard room.'

It was the beginning of the end for Sangret.

'He was a handsome brute,' Greeno recalled, 'stocky, not more than five feet seven inches tall, with a deep chest and massive shoulders tapering to a ballet dancer's waist. His hair was oily black and his face lean and swarthy.'

In his statement, Sangret attempted to explain where Joan might have gone. Perhaps she had run off with a Sudetan Czech named Dworsky or an American called Deadman.

The pathetic pieces of Joan's life found scattered in Houndown Wood during the five days of the statement were now shown to Sangret – the rosary, the red and blue socks, a piece of the green and white dress and her shoes, one with the sole hanging off.

'I guess you have found her,' Sangret said. 'Everything points to me. I guess I shall get the blame.'

Years later, Greeno remembered Sangret shaking and burying his head in his hands. Odd, then, that he did not introduce this possibly damning piece of evidence into his court testimony.

At this point – and for the first time – Greeno confirmed what both men already knew.

'Yes,' he said, 'she is dead.' And he cautioned him in the time-honoured way: 'You are not obliged to say anything, but anything you do say will be taken down and may be used in evidence.'

'She might have killed herself,' the Canadian suggested. It convinced no one.

Years later, and with hindsight, Superintendent Roberts wrote: 'Cunning and guile were evident in all his answers. Self-preservation was his one objective.'

Greeno asked Sangret if he had any bloodstains on his kit. The Canadian gave an emphatic 'No", but the Yard man insisted he change and provide his uniform for forensic tests. Quartermaster-Sergeant Riley passed the kit to Detective Sergeant Hodge who, on 15 October, took it to Dr Roche Lynch at St Mary's Hospital, London. By this time, with nothing incriminating in his 58-page statement, Sangret was visiting his living lady friend in Glasgow. Greeno had nothing to hold him on, but he hoped that science was on his side.

Gerald Roche Lynch was Senior Official Analyst to the Home Office. Educated at St Paul's School, London, he qualified in 1913 and became lecturer in chemical pathology at St Mary's Hospital, Paddington, thirteen years later. 'A fine chemist,' Simpson calls him, but acknowledges him as very much an elder statesman apparently with no life beyond his work and his club. He had held the Home Office post since 1928 and was in 1942 President of the Medico-Legal Society. As a trial witness he was scrupulously careful, completely unruffled. He did not suffer fools gladly and Sergeant Hodge may have been one (as Roche Lynch's obituary in 1957 said) of 'those police officers [who] did not relish orders to deliver materials to his laboratories'. He carried out tests on various articles that he received from the Detective Sergeant. The army trousers and blanket gave the impression of being recently washed. They and the water-bottle gave positive results suggesting the presence of blood, but the washing had effectively made it impossible to confirm that the blood was human. At the trial, Roche Lynch explained that he had first used the benzedine test. This was imperfect because it gave a reaction to things other than blood, such as potassium nitrate and potassium iodine.

The second test was the then new luminescence test, but it had the same flaw, giving a positive in the presence of salts of iron and copper. The fact that *both* tests gave a positive result, however, led him to believe that blood had been present at some stage on trousers and blanket. The cross-examination by Linton Thorp appeared later to veer off at a tangent concerning lice and scabies and Mr Justice Macnaughten, the trial judge, quite rightly brought everybody back to the correct conclusion that science – and Dr Roche Lynch – had effectively let Greeno down. The battledress trousers, the blanket, the water-bottle all belonged to Sangret. Joan Wolfe had probably drunk from the bottle; she had probably wrapped herself in the blanket; but no one could prove that either of them had been covered with her blood.

Greeno did a little experiment of his own. He obtained a WPC of the dead girl's height and wrapped her in Sangret's blanket, marking the policewoman with sticky tape to correspond with Joan's wounds. The tape and the stains on the blanket matched perfectly. Even so, without the *proof* that those stains were blood, Greeno knew he was wasting his time. Had he turned the blanket upside down, of course, none of the stains would have matched anyway.

Two days after these articles were passed to Roche Lynch, Keith Simpson was back in Houndown Wood with Greeno, Webb and Eric Gardner. Together, as he recounted years later in *Forty Years of Murder*, they put together the last seconds of Joan Wolfe's short life.

'I thought it had begun in the dell where Joan's papers were found, probably with the stabbing attack on her head.' This dell is in fact a narrow ravine, its sides higher than Joan wolfe's 5 feet 4 inches. Forestation work and the hurricane of 1987 have cross-crossed the gully with fallen conifers and progress down it is difficult.

> 'She must have run downhill [Simpson conjectured], screaming with pain and fear, inviting pursuit to silence her. Her crucifix ornament must have been torn or pulled away and the contents of her handbag spilled out as she ran. Dizzy and faint because of her head wounds and with blood running from her head wound into her eyes, she was already stumbling at the rivulet, where a tripwire had been laid by exercising troops.'

The rivulet is still there, often dry now, a little trench meandering across a flat valley floor – Houndown Bottom. Lager cans and an odd bucket litter the scene today.

> 'She fell heavily, knocking out her front teeth and further dazing herself, but was almost certainly still able to cry out for help, still inviting a silencing injury. She might have got to her feet, staggered, then fallen again, and was still lying prone, with her right cheek on the ground, when she was struck the final blow with the beech [sic] stake. She must have died

almost immediately. Her killer flung the stake away and then dragged her body into the undergrowth, covering it with a blanket of leaves or both and leaving it ...'

Joan Wolfe died just fifteen paces from the Elstead Road.

But one thing was missing. The first weapon of attack. The knife.

The Canadian Army was issued with knives, but not of the type that tore the ligaments from Joan Wolfe's arm or drilled holes in her head. Despite repeated police searches of the naked woods on Hankley Common, no suitable weapon had been found. Unless of course the rusty blade discovered – and subsequently lost again – by Sergeant Smith had any bearing on the case.

Momentous events were happening overseas. The British Eighth Army stopped Rommel at El Alamein and von Paulus's Sixth Army ground to a frozen halt in the devastated streets of Stalingrad. At Witley Camp, one of the most serious problems was a blocked drain. Private Albert Brown of the Cape Breton Highlanders had the task of sorting it out. On 27 November he shoved his arm down the drain of the shower unit in the guard room, a shower unit which had been dismantled since 9 October. He dragged out paper, cigarette ends, tinsel and a knife. Lance-Corporal Albert Gero saw it too. He opened the clasp and drew then blade across his had to test its sharpness. He stuck it between the pipe and the wall and told Corporal Talbot to show it to Sergeant Wade when he came on duty.

Wade passed it to Sergeant Ballard of the Surrey constabulary and so it reached the Yard. Fingerprint tests were unhelpful. It had after all been immersed in water for a time and handled by at least Brown and Gero and possibly, if he was careless, Ballard. Sergeant Hodge took it to Roche Lynch on 28 November.

The Home Office Analyst subjected the knife to the same tests he had applied to the blanket and to Sangret's battledress trousers. There was no sign of blood or hair on the knife and the scraping he took from the fingernail groove in the blade could not confirm the presence of blood. Neither could he find any trace in the black horn handle, cross-hatched though it was and a perfect surface on which dried blood could collect.

On 3 December, however, Doctors Keith Simpson and Eric Gardner met at Guy's Hospital and came to the independent conclusion that the knife was the weapon involved in Joan's murder. No ordinary knife was the weapon involved in Joan's murder. No ordinary knife could have inflicted muscle injuries of the kind found on Joan's arm. In the trial, Eric Neve for the prosecution was careful to examine the knife's capabilities very thoroughly. Only a blade with a curiously hooked tip could have ripped out ligaments as it was withdrawn; only such a blade could have produced the bevelled circular wounds in the dead girl's skull. Although he could not say positively that this was the weapon in the case, he left it to the jury's sense of coincidence that there should be *two* such knives with a 'parrot's beak'. Neve experimented with the knife while questioning Keith Simpson, whose conclusions were exactly the same as Gardner's.

But whose knife was it? Three Canadian soldiers provided the answer. Samuel Crowle was a private in the Westminster Regiment who had been picking blackberries back in August behind the officers' lines at Camp 103. Near 'a little pile of brush, a shack', he found an army clasp knife with 'a nick right in the front'. It was sticking into the trunk of a tree as though thrown there. He intended to keep it, but Lance-Corporal Ronald Starratt of the Cape Breton Highlanders was an MP and Crowle ended up giving it to him. It was not Canadian issue, Starratt was certain. He had seen its type before when stationed at Bordon in Surrey, to the south-west of the Devil's Punch Bowl. It was rumoured to be British Army issue. Starratt handed it to Corporal Thomas Harding of the Perth Regiment, who put it in a box on his desk. Harding knew for certain that it was British Army issue; he had seen a great many of them hanging on the belts of a great many British soldiers. On Wednesday, 26 August, Sangret came to the guard room to obtain a pass. Harding said to him, 'Here is your knife.' Starratt had told Harding whose knife he thought it was, because of its proximity to the shack. Sangret simply took it, thanked him and pocketed it.

At his trial, Linton Thorp for the defence tried to shake Harding on this point. Harding refused to be shaken. Sangret's defence was that the knife he and Joan used for making the wigwam and for cooking was not Exhibit 4, the knife at the trial. Their knife, he said, had a marlin spike at one end and a can opener. It was Joan's, given to her by her boyfriend Francis. He denied that Harding had given him the knife and when he examined it at the trial, he said he had never seen it before. Confusion arose over the two knives, but Sangret remained adamant that his knife – standard tin-handled Canadian issue – was confiscated by the Military Police and was returned to him. Joan's knife was taken from the tree by the Military Police and had not been returned. Neither of them was the weapon with the hooked beak.

By the time Greeno was ready to see his man again, Sangret had returned from leave and had been posted to Aldershot. It was there, at the Salamanca Barracks, that the second interview took place. In fact, Greeno visited the barracks twice before 6 December, but Sangret was in the sick bay each time and he went away again. In the first interview, Sangret had talked at length about the places the pair had visited. Greeno already knew them well, and any local throughout the days of October and November would have seen little knots of trilby-hatted policemen trudging through the heather and black police cars parked at rakish angles by the roadside. Greeno had crouched beside the makeshift grave of Joan Wolfe; he had stood in the dell where her killer first struck and again on the spot where the birch bough had demolished her skull. Now he wanted to go back to those places with Sangret.

'I should like you, if you will, to accompany me and show me exactly where you mean.'

'All right,' the Canadian had answered.

The visit elicited another statement, Exhibit 45 at the trial. At this stage, Sangret had no idea that Joan's knife had been found.

When they reached the spot on the edge of Hankley Common, where the woods of Houndown moaned dark and wild in the coming of winter, the spot where Joan died, Sangret hesitated, hung back.

'I do not want to go over there,' he said. 'I do not know that place.' He wouldn't even look in that direction. The significance of this will be discussed later.

Sangret signed his second statement. Then, in the presence of Greeno and Hodge, at a little after 4 p.m., he was cautioned by Superintendent Webb and charged officially with the murder of Joan Pearl Wolfe. Such privileges always fall to the local police.

'No, sir,' said Sangret. 'I did not do it. No, sir. Someone did, but I will have to take the rap.'

Sangret was right at least about that.

6

'Fit to Stand His Trial

Christmas came and went. A capital crime like Sangret's would today take eighteen months to come to trial. In the uncertain climate of wartime, the ass that was the law could move faster and on Wednesday, 24 February 1943, in the Surrey Winter Assizes within the County Hall at Kingston upon Thames, August Sangret stood his trial. On the 12 and 13 January, Sangret had appeared at Guildford Petty Sessional Court, having been held on remand at Brixton Prison since 6 December when he was charged with the murder of Joan Wolfe at Thursley during September 1942. Twenty-one witnesses gave evidence, either on this occasion or during the later arraignment on the 19th and 20th, all but one of whom were to do so again, it having been decided that Sangret should 'stand his trial at the forthcoming Surrey Assize Sessions commencing 22 February, 1943, to be holden at Kingston ...'

The previous year, Parliament had passed the United States of America (Visiting Forces) Act which stipulated that military courts tried all cases occurring as a result of their troops being on British soil. The Canadian government made no such decision and accepted the jurisdiction of British courts even in capital cases.

The judge was Sir Malcolm Macnaghten, the fourth son of Baron Macnaghten. His photograph at this time shows a kindly-looking old man with arched eyebrows and a prominent lower lip. He was seventy-four. Like many of his colleagues in the King's Bench Division, Macnaghten had been educated at Eton and Cambridge (Trinity) where he had obtained a first-class honours in the Historical Tripos. A skillful debater, he was President of the Cambridge Union in 1890, was called to the Bar in 1894 at Lincoln's Inn and took silk in 1919. For a time, he was Member of Parliament for North Derry, at a moment in history when that unhappy land was just beginning to settle down after six years of bloody civil war. He had been on the Bench for fifteen years by the time he tried Sangret. He was known as a kindly, courteous man, with more than his fair share of humanity. He made no great mark, but, equally, made few mistakes. Much of his work dealt with Inland Revenue problems and he had been awarded the KBE for his services during the Great War.

Leading for the prosecution was Eric Neve KC, one of the newer breed of lawyers who had gravitated from grammar, rather than public school; he had had a varied background as a private secretary and journalist between 1905 and 1914. During the First World War he served in Palestine and Egypt with the Transport Corps and was called to the Bar at the Middle Temple in 1921. Fifty-six at the time of the trial, he was said to have had one of the best junior practices in the south of England. Even so, Macdonald Critchley, who edited the *Notable British Trials* series, gives no biographical note on him and he doesn't merit more than a few lines in *Who's Who*.

His junior is far better chronicled. He was Geoffrey (later Sir Geoffrey) Lawrence, forty-one years old, the eldest son of a master butcher. His background, like Neve's. Was not run-of-the-mill. Having graduated from New College, Oxford in 1926 with a first-class degree in Jurisprudence, the accomplished pianist and violinist became tutor to the sons of Jan Masaryk, the Czech diplomat who jumped (or was he pushed?) from a window in March 1948 after the Communist takeover of his country. Lawrence was called to the Bar in 1930 but work was hard to get and he had no private means. He was lucky to find Eric Neve, whose practice was thriving; his unusually attractive voice – it was said that he could even make the pattern on the carpet sound interesting – and his superb command of English made him a natural to associate with legal greats like Norman Birkett in the Temple gardens. He had a busy and successful practice of his own by the outbreak of the war and, although silk and his defence of Dr Bodkin Adams lay ahead of him in 1943, he was considered the equal of most barristers of his day. He could lead a 'suspecting – or unsuspecting – witness very politely along a path from the end of which there was no return.'

Sangret was defended by Linton Thorp KC, three years older than Neve. Educated at the now formidable Manchester Grammar School and University College, London, he received a special prize in his final law exams in 1905 and was called to the Bar at Lincoln's Inn in the following year. A major in the Royal Artillery during the First World War, he saw active service, was wounded and spent the early '20s as a judge in Egypt. He was the last British judge of the Supreme Court at Constantinople; then, after 1924, practised at home from Hare Court at the Temple and on the London and South-Eastern circuits. For four years in the hungry '30s he represented Nelson and Colne as Conservative MP. A member of the Carlton Club, he listed his interests in *Who's Who* as 'sailing and outdoor games'.

His junior was Laurence Vine, only months younger than Thorp himself. Like Neve, Vine had been a journalist, working as a reporter or sub-editor on various London and provincial papers. He was called to the Bar at Gray's Inn in 1923, operated on the South-Eastern circuit and listed his hobby as golf.

'August Sangret,' said the Clerk of Assize on that misty Wednesday in late February, 'you are charged for that you, on a day unknown [Greeno always believed it was Monday the 14th] in the month of September 1942, at Thursley in this county, murdered Joan Pearl Wolfe. How say you: are you guilty or not guilty?'

'Not guilty,' answered Sangret.

To the jury, the Clerk said, 'Members of the Jury, the prisoner, August Sangret, is charged that he, on a day unknown in the month of September 1942, at Thursley, in this county, murdered Joan Pearl Wolfe. Upon this indictment he has been arraigned and upon his arraignment he has pleaded that he is not guilty. It is for you to say whether he is guilty or not guilty, and to hearken to the evidence.'

Eric Neve opened for the Crown. He began by reminding the jury of the legality of the situation, that it was up to the prosecution to prove Sangret's guilt beyond a reasonable doubt. He then defined for them the crime of murder:

> 'Murder is the taking by one person of another person's life with malice aforethought. That, put into simple language, is that if anybody commits an act against somebody else by which they die, and that act is committed with the intention of doing an injury which would naturally result in death, that is murder. Malice aforethought merely means intention. In murder you have not necessarily got to have premeditation. It is just as much murder if you strike someone across the head with a log of wood, or stab them, by which they come to their death, if that is done on the spur of the moment, as if you administered poison to them upon a plan with might have taken you weeks or months to perfect.'

Neve then outlined the relationship between the dead girl and Sangret.

> '... she would not perhaps be incorrectly described as somewhat wayward ... She undoubtedly had been mixing with soldiers ... although she undoubtedly should be described as ... wayward ... curiously enough she seems

to have been influenced by strange religious feelings.'

He quoted her letters to the Canadian from hospital and brought the story up to 7 October when the two Marines found Joan's rat-gnawed fingers protruding from her makeshift grave. A book of photographs, bound in blue, was shown to the jury. It showed views of Houndown Woods where the body was found, and the shoes and her other scattered belongings. It showed the decomposing body *in situ*. It showed the dead girl's skull from various angles, with the hole at the back where the birch bough had landed and the curious circular stab wounds at the front. Then Neve showed them Exhibit 3, the murder weapon itself, to which Joan's hair still clung. Then, Exhibit 4, the black-handled knife with the blade like a parrot's beak …

Exhibit 39 was Sangret's statement to Greeno dictated over those five days in October. Neve had only got to the end of July when his voice gave out and Linton Thorp had to take over. The jury must have been heartily glad when they heard the words, 'This statement has been read over to me and it is true, every bit of it, and I understand it. (Signed) August Sangret.'

Seventeen witnesses were called for the prosecution that first day. Inspector Eric Boshier had taken the police photographs, which were referred to as Exhibit 1 in court, of Hankley Common, Thursley cricket green and the guard house at Jasper Camp. Exhibit 2, the blue-bound book of grisly photographs, was produced by the next witness, Tom Roberts, Detective Superintendent in the Surrey constabulary. He also formally produced Exhibit 3, the birch stake murder weapon and Exhibit 4, the knife. Alfred Hassall, of Primrose Ridge, Godalming, was Deputy Divisional Surveyor to Hambledon and testified that Exhibit 48 was an accurate Ordnance Survey map of the Thursley and Witley area of Surrey.

The purpose of these witnesses was simply to establish for the jury that a crime had been committed and to place it in a geographical context. The first 'human' witness was Edith Watts, Joan's mother, whose testimony and whose letters – read out in court – form the bulk of what we know about Joan (see Chapter 3). Exhibit 14 was the crucifix that the girl wore, Exhibit 26 the elephant charm she had given to her. She remembered Exhibit 25, the green purse. All these had been scattered in the dell at Houndown Wood as the terrified girl ran for her life.

Kate Hayter came next. We have already seen that Linton Thorp shook her on dates. The reason for calling her as a witness was to establish in the minds of the jury the physical connection between the dead girl and Sangret. She claimed to have seen them together – although this is unlikely – and certainly established the fact that he came looking for her.

Constable Timothy Halloran was the policeman who had taken Joan and Sangret to the police station in July and had arranged for her to stay in the Church Army hostel in Guildford. He'd seen her again on 23 August at Jasper Camp when Sangret was arrested by the MPs for keeping a girl on army property. It was his sharp memory and accurate pocketbook that led to the rapid identification of the body. Tom Roberts, in *Friends and Villains*, paid him this compliment, '… identification of the victim was solved by the conscientious work of a Godalming beat constable, PC O'Halloran' – pity he got the name wrong!

Sergeant Charles Hicks was the first soldier to give evidence. His involvement with the pair established a microcosm of their relationship for the jury. It was he who read to the illiterate Sangret Joan's letter from Warren Road Hospital of 26 July and it was to him on 27 September that Sangret admitted Joan was missing.

Norah Wheeler, Dorothy Rose, Dorothy Furze and Assistant Matron Margaret Strong all painted a less than flattering picture of Joan during her stay at Warren Road. Mrs Wheeler at least branded her a thief; the matron held that she was an unreliable runaway.

It was the next witness, Private Patrick Anderson, Sangret's bunkmate who told of the row the Métis had had with Joan on the last night he saw her – 'we chewed the fat'. He also established Sangret's sleeping habits, that he was constantly Absent Without Leave, sneaking off with Joan into the woods.

Lance-Corporal Alexander Shearer testified to the living conditions of the lovers and the existence of the ubiquitous 'wigwams' – this particular one on 20 August behind the officers' lines at Witley. His MP colleague, Donald Brett, was the one who found Sangret with Joan's handbag in his kitbag.

Private Samuel Crowle had also come upon a wigwam, which he described as 'a little pile of brush'. He heard people talking inside. This was between 12 and 15 August. On the next day he returned and found Exhibit 4, the knife, 'just stuck in a limb of the tree about 4 feet from the ground and just above the shack'. He intended to keep it, but was persuaded to hand it over to Lance-Corporal Ronald Starratt, of the Military Police, who was the next witness.

Starratt had found Joan in the wigwam on 23 August and had taken her to the guardroom. The next day, Crowle gave him the knife.

Corporal Thomas Harding of the Perth Regiment was the MP in charge of the guard room at Jasper Camp and the last witness to be called on the first day. Sergeant Wade, the Provost-Sergeant, had told him to search the area in August. He found the remains of Sangret's wigwam behind the officers' lines, with parts of a diary and some letters still *in situ*. A second wigwam – 'another grass shack' – he found behind the Sergeants' Mess to the south of the first. Here, with blankets, pack and groundsheet, Harding and his fellow MPs found Joan hiding in the bushes. Starratt in the meantime had passed the knife that Crowle had found to Harding and he put it in a box. It remained there until Wednesday, 26 August when Harding returned it to Sangret, who pocketed it.

At the end of that first day's trial, Mr Justice Macnaghten took the somewhat unusual step of allowing the jury to go home, on the strict understanding of course that they spoke about the case to no one.

Twenty witnesses for the prosecution followed on the second day. The first was Sergeant Harold Wade of the Canadian Grenadier Guards, Greeno's 'wily old warrior' who had served in the Great War. The last time he saw Joan was on 8 September when he was bringing a prisoner back from Bramshot Hospital.

Sangret reported Joan missing to Wade two or three weeks after that. All he had to remember her by at that stage was some pink knitting (evidently Joan believed she was expecting a girl), which he had left with Kate Hayter at Thursley. Sangret had mentioned to Wade snatches of their row the last time he'd seen her: 'I don't think you care whether you marry me or not,' she had said. 'No, I don't,' he'd told her. Wade then told Sangret to forget the girl in that case. The soldier explained that he'd come to report it because if she was found and anything had happened to her, he didn't want to be mixed up in it. He offered to show Wade Kate Hayter's house as he couldn't remember the address. In the event, Sangret never did. It was Wade who had been tipped off by Greeno to hold Sangret in the guard room on 12 October, the day he came to question him.

Robert Talbot, of the Regimental Police under Wade, was a corporal in the Cape Breton Highlanders. He was clearly on reasonably good terms with Sangret as on 12 October, while they were waiting for Greeno to appear, Talbot said, 'I never see you with your girl now.' 'I have not seen her, Bob, for over four weeks,' Sangret had said. She hadn't written to him, nor had she appeared at the old lady's house. It was to Talbot that Sangret confided, 'I have a girl in Scotland and one in Canada; I don't feel like getting married in this country.'

His cross-examination, like that of Wade, revolved largely on the movements in the guard room on 12 October, with particular reference to the wash house next door. Theodore Stiles, Talbot's colleague, faced similar questions.

Major Talmage Gray was in command of the Canadian Educational Company employed as an emergency measure in wartime to bring illiterate and ill-educated soldiers up to a basic standard. Similar units operated in the American armed forces and the sudden awareness of the illiteracy of conscripts had no small connection with the British Education Act of 1944. Gray therefore was, to all intents and purposes, Sangret's commanding officer. He was first made aware of Joan's existence on 24 August when Sangret was brought before him on a charge of keeping a girl on army property. Sangret had told him that he intended to marry her and gray explained the necessary red tape. Oddly, bearing in mind that an education officer was dealing with a man who could only write his name and couldn't read at all, Gray jotted down the essentials on a piece of paper – Exhibit 24 – which was later found fluttering around Houndown Wood. He gave Sangret £1 as he understood that Joan had no means of support. He heard nothing more from Sangret on the subject of marriage.

On 10 October, when he saw him again, Joan was missing. To Gray, Sangret seemed indifferent to that situation.

Private Rudolph Dworsky of the Edmonton Regiment was the Sudeten German to whom Joan had confessed to being German. During the trial it transpired that he was a Czech citizen. He had first seen her sitting near the entrance to Camp 103, knitting. Although he knew that she was going with Sangret – he had seen them together on several occasions – he talked to her at length more than once and arranged to go on walks with her.

Arthur Robinson was the roadman working on Dye House Hill who had seen Joan obviously living in the cricket pavilion at Thursley.

Private Raymond Deadman was the American in the case. He was clearly one of those who had crossed the border into Canada before the 'day of infamy', 7 December 1941, when the United States had been dragged into the war. He does not give his Canadian unit, but was stationed in Thursley Camp early in September while transferring to the 1st Battalion, 133rd Infantry Regiment of the United States Army. Joan by this time was at the cricket pavilion (which Deadman took to be next to a bowling green) and he engaged her in conversation. Sangret arrived and was introduced to him. The next day Deadman visited Joan again and they walked over the common. Sangret turned up again and this time appeared angry that Joan had disobeyed his orders not to leave the 'shack'. These meetings took place on 4 and 5 September. On the 6th, Deadman was posted for duty in Northern Ireland.

The next witness we have heard from already – the ARP Warden William Featherby. He was either highly unobservant (in that he saw no sign of the pair at the pavilion even at two o'clock in the morning) or his dates are hopelessly confused. There seems little doubt that Joan slept there on the last night of her life, although Greeno has another theory on this. The then Chief Inspector believed that Sangret was lying because of Featherby's testimony. The inference is that Joan and Sangret built *another* wigwam, having been moved on from the cricket pavilion, a wigwam perhaps in Houndown Wood. That would put Sangret conveniently near the murder site and not at the pavilion over half a mile away. It would also explain the presence of a worked birch stake in Houndown Bottom – part of the last wigwam which became her murder weapon.

Three of the four children who had seen the couple – and Sangret by himself – were called next. Brother and sister Rita and Derek Bonner of Yew Tree Road, Witley and their friend Grace White, who went to Milford School, remembered the Canadian and his girl looking for rooms for her and blackberrying. They tried to help them, although Sangret's testimony refuted this later. The fourth child, Audrey Saint, was not called, perhaps because she was too young, or because she could add nothing to the testimony of the others. All the children remembered Sangret saying he did not care whether Joan got rooms or not; he was going back to camp.

We have heard already from Alice Curtis of Brook Cottage, Brook, who had seen Joan and a soldier who is likely to have been Sangret wandering the lanes around Witley. She didn't see them after Sunday, 13 September.

With something of a jolt after a civilian interlude, the next witness came again from the army, specifically the North Shore Regiment. Private Joseph Arsenault was stationed at Witley Camp between July and October. He shared Hut E2 with Sangret and noticed him scrubbing his trousers in the washroom after gas treatment. Cross-examination elicited that he couldn't remember when this was. It might have been July, August, September or October.

Company Quartermaster-Sergeant Herbert Riley, of the Educational Company, testified that on 12 October, the day that Greeno first interviewed Sangret, his kit and blankets were handed by him to DS Hodge of the Yard. He testified that Exhibit 34 was a standard, tin-handled Canadian Army issue knife with a spike fitted to the back. Exhibit 4, alleged to be the murder weapon – with its distinctive parrot's beak – was not standard issue, although a similar model *had* been issued to the Canadian army until 1939.

Gunner Frank Dean of the Royal Canadian Artillery remembered writing a letter on Sangret's behalf to a woman in Edinburgh whose name he could not remember on or about 10 October. The purpose of the letter was to arrange to spend Sangret's forthcoming leave with her.

Sapper Clarence Bear of the Canadian Royal Engineers also wrote letters for Sangret; the first to Joan at 'some hospital' in Guildford, bearing the news that he had some money for her and that Major Gray was fixing things up for their marriage. The second letter seems to have been a carbon copy of Dean's. 'It was mostly a love letter,' Bear remembered. 'He wanted to spend his fourteen days' leave with some woman in Glasgow.' Bear had said to Sangret, 'What will Miss Wolfe say if she finds out you are writing to this woman?' Sangret's reply was, 'She will never find out; she has gone on a three weeks' course.'

Joseph Wells was Sangret's friend from Battleford. We have seen already how he helped Sangret look for Joan on the evening of Monday, 14 September. On the 15th, Sangret told him that his water-bottle and knife were missing and he suspected that Joan had taken them 'to build herself a shack or some place in the woods'. On Sunday, 20 September, on the way back from church parade, Sangret suggested that he and Wells go to the pavilion, 'that there was some writing there, and he wanted to see the writing that Joan had left.' Wells pointed out that his reading wasn't up to much. Sangret insisted. 'Between the two of us we might be able to make something out of it.' On the way, Sangret confided to Wells that if 'Joan got sore', she might kill herself. If that was the case, Sangret was afraid that he would be blamed.

Geoffrey Lawrence for the Crown then read out the pathetic ramblings of the dead girl from photographs 12 to 16 in the police dossier. He couldn't decipher the last verse, but Linton Thorp helped him out. 'It is a well known poem:

> The kiss of the sun for pardon,
> The song of the bird for mirth.
> One is nearer to God in a garden
> Than anywhere else on earth.'

Or in a cricket pavilion, perhaps.

Sangret had told the next witness, Private Gilbert Sheppard of the Carleton and York Regiment, before Sheppard had gone on leave on 7 October, that he (Sangret) had sent Joan home because she had run out of clothing coupons.

He had told Private Edward Martineau of the Royal Regiment of Canada that Joan was back in hospital. This would have been about 20 September.

Lieutenant McLeod and Marines Moore and Withington, who had first found the body on the edge of Houndown Wood, were on active service by February 1943 and in accordance with Section 17 of the Defence Regulations, their original depositions were read to the court. The Sangret papers, kindly made available to me by the National Archives of Canada, make it clear that both Scotland Yard and the Joint Surrey constabulary had expressly asked the long list of prosecution witnesses to be held available for the trial if at all possible, irrespective of the need to have them posted elsewhere. The Canadian Army clearly complied.

Sergeant Benjamin Ballard of the Surrey constabulary testified to being the first policeman at the murder scene and to accompanying Joan's body the next day to Guy's Hospital. He itemized the finds made in the careful search on the subsequent days – the tooth, a piece of skull and a tuft of hair; the shoes, scattered; a canvas bag with a rosary; a piece of soap; a water-bottle. And further away, a religious tract, Joan's National Health Insurance card and part of the marriage form, reading 'Proposed wife, date and place of birth', in the handwriting of Major Gray. In a tight little cluster in the dell, the police had found the contents of Joan's handbag – the little white elephant mascot, the crucifix and a copy of the New Testament. The last thing found was Joan's letter to Sangret written from the casualty ward of Warren Road Hospital on 24 August – 'My Dear, well, you can see from my address that I am in hospital again …'

It was Constable Joseph Armstrong, stationed at Witley, who found Exhibit 3, the silver birch stake, in Houndown Bottom. 'When I picked it up, I noticed what appeared to be hair at one end of the stake.' To the rear of the officers' lines at Witley Camp, Armstrong came across a former wigwam – 'a shack built of birch saplings'. Here, on its decaying floor, was a hairpin, a luggage ticket, part of a label marked 'Canadian Red Cross' and two fragments of a letter.

Undoubtedly, though, the star witness was Dr Keith Simpson, the last one to be called that day. Eric Neve knew a performer when he saw one and Simpson played the part to perfection.

Simpson testified that he had got to Hankley Common at about midday on 8 October. The body, that of a woman, was covered, rather than buried, with a thin layer of sandy soil and tilth, varying from 3 inches at its thickest to the merest film.

Mummification had set in in exposed parts like the hand and foot because of the action of the drying air. After careful examination of the body, Simpson had modified his original estimation of the time of death to about one month before the body was found. That would take it to 7 September but the pathologist made it clear that to be that precise was impossible. The last known sighting of Joan was on Sunday, 13 September.

He then explained, with the aid of photographs, the three groups of wounds he had found – the circular stab wounds to the front of the head and the similar wounds to the right forearm (there was no flesh remaining on the left forearm to identify similar wounds there); the blunt injuries to the mouth and face, occasioned either by a blow or a fall; and the oblique hole at the back of the head which represented the fatal blow. The only other wounds on the body were scratches on the lower legs which indicated that the girl's corpse had been dragged through bracken and rough ground.

To Simpson, there was no doubt that the birch stake, Exhibit 3, was the murder weapon. Rather fatuously, Greeno believed that the knife had actually killed Joan, and that the stake was superfluous. He also believed that the circular wounds at the front of Joan's skull were caused by her twisting away. This would have negated any talk of the peculiarities of the knife, as *any* knife would have produced the same wounds. It was as well perhaps for the prosecution that the jury listened to Simpson's theories on this and not Greeno's. The stake fitted exactly with the 1¾ inch wide hole in the skull, and the hairs found clinging to it by PC Armstrong were of the exact type still clinging to the skull itself. Their colour, tint, dimensions and recent evidence of bleaching were determining. Simpson produced a number of micro-photographs of individual hairs to prove his point.

As far as the stab wounds to the front of the skull went, only a knife with the peculiarities of Exhibit 4 could have caused them. Photographs 4A and 4B showed two holes which indicated that a point had been used and a small channel to the right of each hole showed that it had an edge as well. It was a remarkable wound, Simpson said, and the comparison between it and the parrot's beak knife was even more remarkable.

Simpson recalled:

> 'There was a stir is court when I opened my cardboard box. It was one of the few times that a victim's skull had been produced at a murder trial. Knife in one hand and skull in the other, I showed the jury how perfectly the weapon fitted each injury.'

Molly Lefebure, his secretary, remembered it a little differently:

> 'It was the first time a murdered person's skull had ever been produced at a trial. All present craned their necks to see, including the judge; all that is save one, and that one was Sangret. I watched him, but only the merest twinge of curiosity flickered over his face.'

There was a sense of outrage and Linton Thorp particularly protested to the judge. Interestingly, there is no mention of this protest in the official transcript (*Notable British Trials* series).

The court had adjourned for tea as Simpson and Miss Lefebure arrived on that February Thursday. Dr Grierson, Chief Medical Officer at Brixton Prison, invited them to take tea in the gaoler's room, in the dark cellars below the court.

> 'It was a rather grim apartment, with stone floor and bare walls and several cells opening on to it. In the middle of the room was a big wooden table, laid for tea, and the gaoler, one or two policemen, two prison warders and Sangret were standing talking together. We all sat down round the table, with the exception of Sangret

and the warders, who took their tea standing, buffet-style; pretty obviously because Sangret didn't wish to join the tea-party. The atmosphere of the gathering was somewhat out of this world. Dr Simpson, Dr Grierson and the gaoler chatted together on the subject of juries. The policemen were discussing football. I couldn't overhear the conversation between Sangret and the warders, but it sounded amiable enough. I sat silent, eating bread and butter and drinking good, hot, thick tea from an even thicker cup. Every now and again I tried to stare at Sangret without staring at him … although he was not a very sensitive-looking man, I did not like to stare at him too much. So I sat quietly sipping tea and listening to the conversation about juries on the one hand, the conversation about who was going to be top of the league on the other, and wondering what Sangret and the warders were talking about. It certainly was the strangest tea-party I ever went to.'

The third day of the trial began with more forensic evidence, this time from Dr Eric Gardner. There was a discrepancy between his findings and those of Simpson which Linton Thorp could work on. Even so, Linton Thorp was furious with Simpson for bringing the actual skull into court when photographs (which had been shown already to the jury) would have done perfectly well. Nothing of the 'truculent and perhaps uneasy counsel' is evident in the flat prose of the trial transcript, but Macdonald Critchley, writing in 1957, quotes the judge in his summing up, referring to Linton Thorp's 'duel with the doctors'. Interestingly, Keith Simpson thought that it was the judge who was unimpressed by his findings on the knife wounds to the skull, rather than the defence.

Eric Gardner had a medical practice at Weybridge and was Consulting Pathologist to the hospital there. He agreed with Simpson, after the post-mortem on the rotting corpse, that it had lain under its light tilth for about a month. He had worked out the rate of decomposition based on the mean daily temperatures in September and October. There was no excessive heat during that period so that decomposition advanced at the normal rate for that time of the year. The fact that two bucketsful of maggots had been removed from the body cavity during the post-mortem implied that the corpse had lain elsewhere for a time, unburied, between death and its final interment on the high ground above Houndown Wood. Further, the underside (front) of the body was warm because of the generation of heat by the feeding maggots.

As to the wounds, the peculiar knife, Exhibit 4, had caused them. And the blanket, Exhibit 47, was stained with what could well be Joan's blood, which would have gone on oozing into the fibres for a day or so after death, simply by the force of gravity. It was clearly quite impossible for any of the blows to have been self-inflicted.

There was much cross-examination concerning mummification, the temperature at which maggots thrived, the angle of the stake as it struck the girl's head and the knife wounds and the amount of blood such wounds would be likely to produce.

Dr Roche Lynch followed with his evidence of tests on Sangret's battledress, blanket, water-bottle and hook-bladed knife. Roche Lynch got the impression that Sangret's battledress trousers and army blanket had recently been washed – the water-bottle had not. Because of the tests he had used, he came to the conclusion – and he confessed to not being certain – that there had been blood on both. Even on the knife, he could not be sure: 'All I can say is that there may have been blood there, but I cannot prove it.' He had made cuts in the knife handle, which a couple of earlier witnesses were a little confused by, but even so they had not yielded the positive results the police expected.

Linton Thorp attempted to suggest that the positive bloodstains Roche Lynch did get from the blanket may have been caused by scratching because of lice infestation. Joan was likely to have been lousy and it was possible that Sangret was. Justice Macnaghten interrupted at this point to say that, in effect, cross-examination was unnecessary, as 'there is no evidence that there was any blood upon this man' (Sangret).

The next witness was Sergeant James Smith of the Surrey constabulary who emerged in rather a poor light and was to be recalled on the fourth day of the trial. On the afternoon of 9 October, he had been searching Hankley Common and Houndown Wood and found a knife similar to Exhibit 34, the tin-handled Canadian Army issue. Believing it to be irrelevant to the case, he threw it away. He found it near the Royal Marine Camp 'at the top of the hill' (where precisely this was, I am unable to say). Linton Thorp badgered the man for his stupidity and bad practice and not even Justice Macnaghten's intervention could save him: 'He has answered your question; he said he thought it had nothing to do with the job. That is a perfectly good answer.' 'Yes, my lord,' Linton Thorp humoured the old man, 'it is a perfectly good answer, but perhaps a perfectly bad reason.' Macnaghten conceded that he had a point.

The knife was never found. It still lies, rusty and silent, keeping its secret, somewhere in Houndown Wood.

Constable Brian Gunning was then called to testify to finding various items behind Thursley cricket pavilion – a pair of stockings, a black garter, a knitting instruction booklet and four pieces of sacking.

Four soldiers, three of them MPs – Private Samuel King of the Royal Canadian Engineers, Lance-Corporal Albert Gero of the Cape Breton Highlanders, Private Albert Brown of the same regiment and Thomas Harding, who was recalled – testified to the finding of the knife in the blocked drain. Then Chief Inspector Greeno took the stand. He outlined his involvement in the case from the time the Chief Constable of Surrey had called in the Yard to the day he let Superintendent

Webb arrest Sangret for Joan's murder. Greeno was sweating a little throughout this testimony. He had kept Sangret for five days – four days longer than the law of habeas corpus allowed – while he made his statement back in October. Sir Norman Kendal had rung him, worried, on this very point. Seventeen years later, Greeno was smug that defence counsel failed to raise the issue. A 'pickier' court may have flung out the prosecution case then and there.

Detective Sergeant Hodge had been allowed to stay in court during Greeno's testimony; he merely explained details of the passing on of artefacts to Roche Lynch and the forensic team, and agreed that Sangret's statements were in his handwriting.

Superintendent Webb gave his testimony, which mirrored Greeno's entirely and concluded with his arrest of Sangret. 'No, sir,' the Canadian had said. 'I did not do it. Somebody did it, but I will have to take the rap.' 'That,' said Eric Neve, 'is the case for the Crown.'

There was only one witness for the defence, as opposed to fifty-two for the prosecution – August Sangret himself – and Thorp called him to the stand. He talked him through his whirlwind courtship with Joan Wolfe. He read her letters to the court. They had got to 1 September by the end of the day's proceedings. The weekend intervened, during which, presumably, the jury were once again allowed to go home.

On Monday, 1 March, Linton Thorp resumed. He took the story up to Greeno's second meeting with Sangret, then allowed Eric Neve to cross-examine. One of the problems in piecing together the Sangret case is that the trial itself excited little public interest at that time. There was a war on. Even paper was scarce. In North Africa, Rommel was in retreat before the Eighth Army; in Russia, the Red Army was winning back its towns from a retreating *Wehrmacht*. At home, Labour MPs Nye Bevan and Manny Shinwell were demanding immediate implementation of a welfare state. Against all this, the fate of an obscure Canadian paled into relative insignificance. It takes a little imagination therefore to see the fire in Neve's attack from the dead print on the page. In a barrage of questions, he went for Sangret, bombarding him with all the inconsistencies of his story.

'Did he [Mr Featherby, the ARP warden] not tell you that you and Joan were not allowed to live in the pavilion?' … 'He has denied that. He is quite wrong that he emphatically told you you could that night and no longer, is he?' … 'He has said that he did. If he came at two o'clock in the morning, if what you are saying is true, you must have been there?' and so on. How rattled Sangret became, how easily he answered questions, it is now not possible to say. Only in his summing up did Mr Justice Macnaghten hint at Sangret's problem. It will be discussed later.

At the end of the fourth day of the trial, the unfortunate Sergeant Smith was recalled. Linton Thorp was still chasing him about the discarded knife. The policeman made it clear that it was standard Canadian issue, unlike the supposed murder weapon, Exhibit 4. Then prosecution and defence counsels addressed the jury. Curiously (and it is an unfortunate problem), no transcript of either address has survived. We therefore are in a more difficult position than the jury because we have to sift the evidence ourselves and come to our own conclusions. On the positive side, we cannot be swayed by the rhetoric of advocacy either, so it may be a blessing in disguise.

On the fifth day, Tuesday, 2 March, Mr Justice Macnaghten delivered his summing up.

> 'That the girl was murdered is not in dispute; that she was murdered by some man is also quite plain; and the only question you have to determine is: Have the Crown satisfied you beyond all real doubt that the prisoner, August Sangret, is the man who murdered her?'

It was a model of impartiality and it ended:

'I can only conclude by saying what I said at the beginning: when dealing with a case of circumstantial evidence you must be satisfied beyond all real doubt before you find that the prisoner is guilty. If you come to the conclusion that, on the facts proved before you, no real doubt is left in your minds that his was the hand which slew this unhappy girl, then you will convict him. Let the Bailiffs be sworn.'

At 12.55 p.m. the jury retired to consider their verdict. They took with them the knife of August Sangret and the skull of Joan Pearl Wolfe.

The *circumstantial* evidence against Sangret seemed overwhelming and the twelve men and true found him 'guilty, but with a strong recommendation to mercy', in a verdict delivered at 2.55 p.m. on Tuesday, 2 March 1943.

One of the weaknesses of the jury system, in Britain at least, is that the outside world is not privy to the jury's discussions behind closed doors. It is a maxim of English law that a man has the right to be tried by a jury of his peers. It is debatable of course whether these twelve English men and women were *actually* the peers of a half-breed Canadian Indian nearly 5,000 miles away from home. Neither Eric Neve nor Geoffrey Lawrence for the Crown, nor Linton Thorp nor Laurence Vine for the defence ever, as far as I know, went into print on the behaviour of the jury in this case, or indeed into the case at all. Those who have, like Keith Simpson and Molly Lefebure, concentrate inevitably on the forensic involved, or like Ted Greeno, congratulate themselves on a job well done. I have had no communication from any members of that jury. Did they consider other suspects in the man-filled life of Joan Wolfe? Were they happy with the forensic and police cases before them? Did they feel sorry for the 'handsome brute' who was the Prisoner at the Bar? Neither Keith Simpson nor Molly Lefebure could understand the recommendation to mercy. Perhaps with the distance of hindsight, we can.

'August Sangret [said the judge, grave and black-capped], the jury have found that it was you who murdered Joan Wolfe and none who heard the evidence can doubt the justice of the verdict. They have accompanied it with a strong recommendation for mercy; that will be forwarded to the proper quarter. It only remains for me to pronounce the sentence prescribed by law.

The sentence of the court is that you be taken from here to the place from whence you came, and from there to a place of lawful execution, and that there you be hanged by the neck until you be dead; and that your body afterwards be buried within the confines of the prison in which you shall have been last confined. And may the Lord have mercy on your soul.'

Seconds before Macnaghten delivered these dull, deadly, yet electrifying words, Sangret had been asked by the Clerk of the Court if he had anything to say.

'I am not guilty, sir,' he answered. 'I never killed that girl.'

7

Métis

Battleford, Saskatchewan stands on the Battle River some 50 miles south-east of Maidstone and 70 miles north-west of Saskatoon, in the mid-west of Canada. The area marks the northern limit of the Great Plains, scene of that last frontier which has captured the hearts and imaginations of generations of men for over one hundred years. The names Saskatchewan (meaning 'rapid river') and Saskatoon (a local edible berry) come from the language of the Cree Indians, to whose people August Sangret belonged.

A solitary railway line runs along the North Saskatchewan River, west of North Battleford. Beyond it the plains stretch on, it seems, for ever, flat and brown in the autumn. Only clumps of trees break the horizon; low, stunted stands of silver birch. Here it is exposed, lonely, the only sound the moan of the wind in the trees.

The Cree are one of the major Algonkian-speaking peoples who expanded rapidly in the seventeenth and eighteenth centuries to occupy a huge area between Hudson Bay and James Bay in the east and Alberta and the Great Slave Lake in the west. They shared the huge area with the Blackfeet and Assiniboine, the Plains Ojibwa, the Gros Ventre and the Sarcee. They were numbered among that group called by Lewis and Clark in 1805 'the roving Indians of Sascatchewain'. The name Cree is a contraction of the French Kristineaux, which seems to be a form of the tribe's name for itself, though the meaning is now lost. The coming of the white man brought firearms, a brisk trade in furs and smallpox on an unprecedented scale. Wars with neighbouring tribes of the Blackfeet and Dakota to the south contributed to a reduction in numbers, so that today, only about 200,000 survive on reserves.

Sociologically, the Cree are divided into two groups – the woodland or Swampy Cree and the Plains Cree. From the discussion of him by contemporaries like Macdonald Critchley, Sangret's forebears probably belonged to the former, although with the coming of the white man with his treaties and reserves, the distinction became impossibly blurred. The Woodland group hunted caribou, moose, bears, beaver and hares. They were forest dwellers, living in lodges or tipis made of brush and leaves. Their homes were domed or beehive-shaped lodges of willow poles, arched so that both ends entered the ground, and were covered with birch bark. At the centre of these wigwams was the fireplace in typical constructions, but sometimes the more easterly Cree made *shabuktowan* – 'the house that you walk right through' – with an entrance and exit and a fire at each end. Such wigwams were built by placing two poles on the ground in the form of a cross. Then a third was added and lashed to the others before being hauled upright to form a tripod. Sheets of silver birch bark, 3 feet wide, were stretched over the frame. Far from the primitive 'dens' we all made as children out of grass and a lot of imagination, these wigwams were sturdy and well constructed. And they were made with a pointed awl and a small crooked knife, a tool unique to the Cree. This was the principal construction method of the Ojibwa and Algonquin tribes as well as the Cree who, with a less well-defined social structure, borrowed ideas extensively from both. The climate was wrong for the growing of maize, so famine was frequent. Their social organization was based on bands composed of related family groups, although for war they amalgamated to form larger bands. They were a deeply superstitious people.

Battleford lies to the south of the area known as the Interior Plains. Whatever the sociological origins of Sangret's Cree ancestors, by the time his grandparents were born, that area had been the hunting grounds of the nomadic Plains Cree for generations. In keeping with the better known tribes of North America, the Sioux and the Cheyenne, the Cree hunted the American bison or buffalo, using every part of the animal for their survival. Its meat was cured over smoky fires and eaten in the harsh winter months as pemmican. Its hide was stretched over lodge poles to make tipis or wigwams. The rough edge of its tongue was a comb for long, black hair. Its belly sac was a bucket. Its bones were boiled down with its hoofs to make glue – rather as the people of Britain were doing to weld aircraft parts in the war. The Cree were known to be amongst the most skilful hunters on the continent and scorned neighbouring tribes like the Chippewa whose proficiency lay largely in fishing. But even the Cree gathered along river banks and the lake shores in the summer where the swarms of blackfly and mosquitoes were less of a plague.

The Plains Cree wore shirts and leggings of buffalo and deer skin. They used beads as ornaments. The colour white (the colour of Joan Wolfe's elephant mascot) typified peace, prosperity and goodwill. The colour purple (the colour of the heather on Hankley Common) spoke of war, disaster and death. And Cree men and women carried (like Joan Wolfe) a medicine bag to ward off evil.

In common with the other Plains tribes, the Cree worshipped the Great Spirit whose most visible signs were the sun and the thunder. The great religious occasions of the year were the Sun Dance and the Horse Dance when offerings of tobacco smoke were made as presents to the Great Spirit. Each Cree believed that a supernatural power watched over him, aware of every action, ready to help in times of crisis. Such powerful medicine became diluted on contact with the vastly more numerous white man whose Christianity threatened their souls as surely as his rifle threatened their livelihood. Bears held a particularly powerful place in Cree mythology. A bear's skull was the most prized of possessions – kept, preserved and decorated as an offering to animal spirits. Rather as Joan Wolfe's skull was 'decorated' with wire to restore it; rather as it was kept and preserved at Guy's Hospital, and as it was offered for the first time in an English courtroom to the gasps of onlookers and in the name of the spirit of truth.

The Cree were a warlike people, each camp run by an elite military society composed of the bravest men in the twenty-five to thirty-five age group. When, for instance, the tribe rose up in 1885 under Poundmaker, it was the Rattlers, a kind of internal military police, who took over the running of the camp under their out-spoken, short-tempered leader, Wandering Spirit. It was this tradition that made it natural for August Sangret to become a soldier, even before war broke out.

During food shortages, when the caribou, buffalo and hares were scarce, starvation was rife and there are examples of cannibalism which horrified Indian contemporaries as much as it does us. The superstitions of the Cree were such that they were terrified of witchcraft and shamans and conjurors wielded enormous power, often overriding the counsel of chiefs. As in medieval Europe, the horned god held great supernatural powers. The Cree were at one with nature. The winds were four brothers, the oldest and wisest the North Wind who brought the cold and punished evil doers. The spirits of the Cree ancestors lived on in the forms of the animals they hunted. Out of the combination of cannibalism and the occult were born the Wendigo, human beings transformed into supernatural man-eating giants through eating human flesh. They were creatures of the forest, prowling the silver birches, and one wonders if, in his darkest moments, August Sangret did not see in Chief Inspector Greeno the Wendigo of his childhood, not crashing through the tree-stands on the plains to swallow him whole, but arriving at Jasper Camp, Witley, in a plain, black Railton car.

As far as women were concerned, the females of the Cree were considered the most attractive of the Plains Indians. One of the witnesses at Sangret's trial complained that the man treated Joan 'like a goddam squaw'. Certainly, women were subordinate to men. No woman was allowed to step over a hunter's legs as he sat by the fire. But conversely, women were held in a certain awe because childbirth was a powerful mystery. Sangret may have used contemporary Canadian jargon to describe Joan's menstrual state – she should have had the 'flag flying', but had not 'come on' – but the fact that he seems to have accepted that her baby was his shows a lamentable lack of knowledge of elementary physiology.

European involvement in Saskatchewan began in 1691 with Henry Kelsey, the first white man known to have set foot in the area, on behalf of the Hudson's Bay Company. This company, with four beavers sejant on its coat of arms, was originally the gift of Charles II to his cousin, Rupert of the Rhine, and seventeen other noblemen for 'the sole trade and commerce of all those seas, straits, bays, rivers, lakes, creeks and sounds … that lie within the entrance of the strait commonly called Hudson …' In its endless search for valuable furs and pelts, the company spread ever westward, trading with the Indians and intermarrying with then, clashing with the trappers of the French Compagnie du Nord who were particularly taken with the beautiful Cree women. Although the area became the property of the British Crown in 1869 and one year later part of the new Dominion of Canada, it was thick with Frenchmen, part of the earlier legacy of France's settlement of Canada and North America generally.

The railway brought further Europeans in 1882, by which time the 'Cree had degenerated', according to Diamond Jenness in 1967, 'and were no longer the adventurous hunters and warriors who had traversed hald the Dominion. The white man's liquor and the white man's diseases had left their mark . . . and the Cree suffered heavily from epidemics of influenza in 1908 and 1909 and again in 1917 . . . the pitying scorn of the white man destroys their morale and robs them of self-respect and pride of race.'

No doubt there was originally an element of sincerity in the whites' dealing with the Cree. Lieutenant-Governor Archibald in a speech in Manitoba in July 1871 said:

'Your Great Mother [Victoria] wishes the good of all races under her sway. She wishes her red children to be happy and contented. She would like them to adopt the habits of the white, to till the land, raise food and store it up against a time of want. She thinks this would be the best thing for her red children to do, that it would make them safer from famine and distress and make their homes more comfortable …'

The Crees seemed to have largely accepted this concern and signed away their birthright. It could be argued that they had little choice. The way of the plains and the buffalo was rapidly vanishing. In the early 1870s an average 5,000 buffalo a *day* were being killed by white hunters. By 1883 perhaps only 1,000 were left in the whole North American continent. So it was that the Cree chief Pehtokahanopewin (Poundmaker) agreed reluctantly in 1878 to Treaty Number 6 which effectively reduced his people to third-rate farmers without skill or inclination. The 'experts' put on the reserves by whites to help them were as unconcerned or full of self-interest as the various agents who ran the reserves. Fire swept the plains in the late '70s, bringing death on an unprecedented scale to the wildlife. The Cree way of life died with it. They became, in the words of modern writers Jean Goodwill and Norma Sluman, 'a silent and shattered people'.

Conflict came, when it did, not from a direct clash between Indians and whites, but from a group of half-breeds known to the Canadians as Métis. These fiercely proud nomads of mixed Indian and French parentage were also known as the '*bois brûlé*', the burnt wood people, because of the colour of their faces. The Plains Indians called them 'Wagon men' and in their sign language to each other circled their thumbs and index fingers to form the shape of the wheels of their famous Red River carts. The Métis on the move could be heard miles away because of these vehicles. The incessant yellow summer dust clung to greased axles and wore them down, so the Métis used no grease. The resultant noise was likened to 'a thousand fingernails drawn across a thousand panes of glass'. One of their permanent trackways, from which Canada's modern motorways were formed, ran from Batoche through Battleborough, Fort Carlton and on to Edmonton.

Although they lived by mixed farming, and clashed with the nomadic Lakota or Sioux tribes from the south, who recognized no artificial frontier such as the American-Canadian border, the Métis followed their Indian heritage and hunted the buffalo. In June and September, until there were no more buffalo to hunt, they rode on to the plains in their moccasins and fringed buckskins to follow a rigid etiquette of slaughter, 'the coursers rearing, neighing, dancing, digging at the ground with eager hooves'. It was as much a part of their culture as it was of the Indians' and they found no difficulty in squaring that with their devout Catholicism.

In the 1840s, the Saskatchewan river area, with its biggest Métis settlement at Batoche, was still a wilderness. Even forty years later, Big Bear's Crees could still vanish into this vast emptiness with little chance of a white man finding them. The Métis, at an estimated 5,000, outnumbered the white population ten to one. An English traveller noted that they were 'a fine race, tall, straight, well-proportioned, lightly formed and extremely active ... Their chests, shoulders and waists are of that symmetrical shape so seldom found among the broad-waisted, short-necked English or the flat-chested, long-necked Scotch.'

They had common French surnames like Boucher, Bois-Bert, Dumas, Goulet, Lucier, Martel and Villebrun and they spoke a patois oddly fixed in the late eighteenth century which increasingly lost pace alongside the developing French language of the Québécois, the French-speaking Canadians to the east.

Historically, there was no love lost between the French-Catholic Métis and the increasing numbers of Presbyterian Scots who began to trickle into the Red River and Saskatchewan areas as a result of the Highland clearances of 1812. The Governor of the wilderness than was Miles Macdonald and the owner the Earl of Selkirk. The Métis were forbidden to hunt on horseback or to see their wares without Scottish permission. This hostility led to the only instance of savagery by the Métis when, on 19 June 1816, Scots settlers were butchered by a Métis war party.

In the increasing aggression from the endless spread of settlers to the west, and in the increasing indifference to the Métis position by the Ottawa government, the half-breeds found a leader in 'the miller of the seine', Louis Riel, whom the Hudson's Bay Company had refused permission to set up his own woollen mill.

The creation of the Dominion of Canada in 1870, welding the four provinces of New Brunswick, Nova Scotia, Ontario and Quebec into one, only worsened the poor Métis-white relationship. Rupert's land was bought for £300,000 by the new government, but the wishes of the Métis were ignored. Louis Riel, who had led his people for nearly twenty years, was dead, and the new immigrants arriving in the area – the 'Canada Firsters' – were largely Protestant Orangemen, opposed by faith and race to the Indians and the Métis.

The mixed farming of the Métis involved the tenure of long strips of land called River or Quebec lots which incorporated where possible river banks, woodland and open prairie, the latter held in common as the 'hay privilege'.

It was Louis Riel's son, also Louis, who held out for the preservation of this way of life. One-eighth Chippewa, Riel was less Indian than most of the Métis and a man of articulacy and vision. Backed by about 6,000 French-speaking half-breeds, Riel produced a 'List of Rights' for the Council of Assiniboia, which demanded prior consultation with the Métis, a voice in the democratic process (the Métis had no vote) and government protection of land, religion and language. The

Métis established their own short-lived local government, and the obsolete fleur-de-lis flag of the Bourbons fluttered for a while over Fort Garry.

By May 1870, the Manitoba Act gave substance to Riel's List of Rights and it seemed that justice and liberality had won the day. By a secret codicil, however, 1,200 troops were to be stationed in the area, and Riel fled for safety to the United States.

As with treaties made with the Indians, the terms of the Manitoba Act collapsed under the weight of increasing westward expansion. The government saw the Métis as squatters, an obsolete inconvenience to the creation of a modern nation-state. Surveyors drew up American-style grids that gave them rights to *squares* of land, not their river-strips, and that only after a three-year period before patents (deeds) were granted. By 1880, the exiled Riel was allowed to return and he sent an official protest to Ottawa. It was ignored.

Over the next five years, the Métis rode headlong into a confrontation that was to lead to the end of their independence and of their dream. Louis Riel was becoming increasingly irrational and had mystical visions. He spent a few years in asylums. Others saw him as 'a Joshua, a prophet, even a saint'. He saw himself as a Messiah.

And inexorably, the government of John Macdonald – 'Old Tomorrow' – moved against him. The Mounted Police contingent at Fort Carlton, 20 miles from Batoche, was reinforced. By March 1885, Riel was tired of waiting – 'We are going to take up arms for the glory of God, the honour of religion and for the salvation of our souls.' And God appeared to the Métis when the dark covered the sun in a partial eclipse. The 400 cavalry of Riel's provisional government of the Saskatchewan was composed of hard-bitten hunters and led by the brilliant Gabriel Dumont. They easily overawed the fifty 'Mounties' and offered them safe conduct out of Fort Carlton.

But time and progress were not on Riel's side. The mere existence of the North-west Mounted Police, created in 1873, was testimony to that. And the Canadian Pacific Railway was creeping westward, bringing with it civilization, law and technology. The clash came at Duck Lake where Major Leif Crozier's Mounties complete with volunteers, a field piece and twenty horse-drawn sleighs, fell into a typical Dumont trap. After half an hour, five of the rebels were dead and three wounded, but the Canadians had suffered more – twelve dead and eleven wounded. It was Riel who had prevented it from being any worse, riding in front of his sharpshooters: 'For the love of God, kill not more of them.' The Métis helped the Mounties load their dead onto a cart.

And now the sides gathered. Riel sent messages to his 'dear relatives', the Indians. The worry for the government and the white settlers was that there were 20,000 Indians on the plains, increasingly near to the end of their tether because of shortage of rations and the wholesale slaughter of the buffalo. What if Riel's incitement to rebellion provided the snapping of that tether? And the signs looked ominous. At Battleford, Poundmaker with his 200 Cree warriors, painted terrifyingly for war, sacked the stores and danced and sang in the streets, grotesquely draped in ladies' frocks, courtesy of the Hudson's Bay Company. Furniture was smashed and the starving Crees took food back to their people. The whites hid in the fort-like barracks nearby with the garrison of forty-three Mounties. At Fort Pitt on Frog Lake, Big Bear's Crees attacked the thirteen white settlers and the yellow-painted Wandering Spirit shot the Indian agent, Tom Quinn.

There was panic in Ottawa and the new nation flexed its muscles for the first time. Montreal sent its Garrison Artillery, the French-speaking 65th Rifles and the 9th Voltigeurs. Ontario sent the 7th Fusiliers, the Royal Grenadiers and the Queen's Own Rifles. Nova Scotia fielded the Halifax Battalion, and Manitoba, the 90th Infantry Battalion and the 91st and Light Infantry Regiments. In the west, where there was less order and more improvisation, white settlers quickly scrambled together units like the Rocky Mountain Rangers and the Moose Mountain Scouts. In the early spring of 1885, over 8,000 men were marching, with nine field pieces and two experimental

American Gatlings that fired at the horrific rate of 1,200 rounds a minute. And Ottawa bought off the Indians to ensure that Poundmaker's and Big Bear's bands were the only ones to back Riel. Huge supplies of flour, tea, beef and tobacco rattled westward on the new railway to the reserves of the Blackfeet, the Stoney and the Salteaux.

The campaign was hard. In temperatures of 65 degrees below freezing, men's toes and fingers fell victim to frostbite. In the fierce glare of the ineffectual sun, they went blind. Marching at night was as bad. They became disoriented in the dark. Some of them went mad. The attack was to be three-pronged, an unfortunate echo perhaps of Custer's attack on the Lakota and Cheyenne on the Big Horn miles to the south and nine years earlier. The main force under the unimaginative Major-General Frederick Middleton was to march from Qu'Appelle to Batoche, but the man was a great believer in infantry and his ponderous column managed only 150 miles in three weeks. His cavalry hovered at the rear, protecting the baggage and the railway from the lightning attacks he knew the Métis could launch.

Dumont hit them at Fish Creek, firing uphill (a tactic no European-trained soldier would attempt) from hidden ravines, picking off the Canadians like ducks in a shooting gallery, silhouetted against the sky. Middleton couldn't depress his cannon to a steep enough angle to reply with shrapnel and his bayonet charges were beaten back by merciless rifle-fire. The Métis, outnumbered five to one, took up their 'Falcon song' to the accompaniment of a flute. The ambush resulted in fifty-five of Middleton's men dead or wounded for only four Métis casualties. And the army's advance was stopped dead. The second prong was led by Colonel William Otter, later to distinguish himself in the Boer War, from Swift Current to Battleford. His force consisted of 325 soldiers, including seventy-five Mounties, two 7-pounder cannon and a Gatling. He hit Poundmaker's Crees at Cut Knife Creek, but the shells that tore holes in the tipis achieved little else. Three hundred Indians, armed with obsolete rifles, bows and arrows, fought

Otter's well-armed troops to a standstill and almost wiped out his command before they let him crawl away.

After two weeks of indecision, Middleton pulled himself and his force together and launched a double attack on Batoche, in reality only a large village with its back to the South Saskatchewan River. The first offensive was by river, as the steamer *Northcote* chugged its way upstream, loaded with troops and cannon. The wily Dumont was ready, however, and two ferry cables were pulled across the steamer's path, ripping off its masts and funnels to make it unusable in a military capacity again. When the infantry assault began, Dumont's sharpshooters again opened fire from hiding. The Canadians pulled back, grateful for the cover of night, to their zoreba or stockade of wagons.

Once again, Middleton hesitated. He had 900 men to Dumont's 300, but the accuracy of the Métis had unnerved him. In the end, Colonel Williams of Ontario broke the General's order and led an assault, other units joining him. The Métis fought doggedly, scrambling back from one trench to another in an orderly retreat. Their rifles now fired nails, buttons, even pebbles after their ammunition ran out. One of the dead was ninety-three-year-old Joseph Ouellette who refused to leave his trench: 'Wait, I want to kill another Englishman.'

But it was over. The third prong of the attack, led by Major-General Thomas Strange from Calgary to Edmonton, there to join Middleton, was specifically in revenge for the Cree attacks. To his astonishment, he found his cavalry outmanoeuvred by the Crees and pulled back, not wishing, in his own words, to 'commit Custer'. On 3 June, Middleton caught up with him and the Crees were defeated at Loon Lake, with heavy casualties on the Canadian side. Over the next weeks, white hostages were returned unharmed and the starving Crees surrendered.

What did it all add up to, the most serious rebellion ever faced by the Canadian government and people? Riel's rebellion had cost an estimated $5 million, a sum the fragile new government could not really afford. Eighteen Métis were tried, convicted of treason and sentenced to seven years in prison. Eleven Indians were due to be hanged at Battleford on the same day, but three were reprieved. For reasons of liberality and politics, Poundmaker and Big Bear, the Cree chiefs, were given three years each. Both of them died within six months of their release, broken in health and spirit.

Dumont escaped from the trenches at Batoche and refused to surrender. He reached the safety of Montana, where his descendants live to this day. He was to ride with William F Cody's Wild West Show into a glorious sunset that marked the end of an era. Louis Riel could be allowed no such escape. Surrendering to the Mounties, he was tried at Regina, the provincial capital, accused of treason and incitement to rebellion. His four-man team of lawyers pleaded insanity – 'megalomania, the mania of ambition' – but Riel would not hear of it.

'When I came here,' he said, 'I found the Indians starving. The half-breeds were subsisting on the rotten pork of the Hudson's Bay Company.'

He emerged as a noble, if unstable, leader of his people driven to desperate measures by a callous and uncaring government. The jury took an hour and twenty minutes to find him guilty, but, in an interesting reflection of the Sangret case, the jury foreman, Francis Cosgrove, said, 'Your Honour, I have been asked by my brother jurors to recommend the prisoner to the mercy of the Crown.'

French-Canadians applauded this, but others did not. 'We consider,' sneered the Protestant *Selkirk Herald*, 'that such lives as that of Riel are blots and stains on our humanity . . .'

They hanged Louis Riel, the Joshua, the Messiah, on 16 November 1885 in Regina as the prison chaplain intoned the words of the Lord's Prayer.

Two hundred miles away, in Battleford, there lived a four-year-old Métis boy called Napoleon Sangret.

We do not know what part, if any, the Sangrets played in Riel's rebellion. My letter to an 'L Sangret' listed in Battleford today elicited no reply. We are left, then, with conjecture. Poundmaker's Crees, as we have seen, sacked Battleford in a scene which it is likely the little Napoleon, if indeed he lived there then, would have witnessed. The Cree were the Métis' allies and therefore probably in no danger from then. It is not likely, then, that the Sangrets were huddled in the Mounties' fort for safety.

Whether the Sangret family was involved in the rebellion has no lasting significance because, after 1885, the same fate befell *all* Métis. Only the Métis of Saskatchewan had joined Riel, however, and perhaps white Canadians were to remember that for a long time to come.

The Métis would never stand and fight again. Some fled west, changing their tell-tale names and following game in the nomadic ways of their ancestors. Others took the Saskatchewan River to the north. Dumont's followers, the dogged cavalry of Batoche, were accepted in Montana as political refugees by the American President, Grover Cleveland. Still others worked on the ever-spreading railway of the Canadian Pacific.

It is likely, because of the Sangret association with Battleford, that the family was one on those who stayed put in the hope that the Ottawa government would forgive and forget. A land grant scheme known as 'scrip' was devised for settled Métis, which in effect acknowledged the justice of Riel's demands prior to 1885. Money scrip, worth $240, was more alluring than land scrip, however, and starving, sick families took this offer readily. They then realized that its actual value was only half its face value and that, by accepting it, they had given up rights to the land. Such families quickly became part-time agricultural workers, squatting on scrub land the whites did not want.

Their work was hard and their pay abysmal. They repaired fences in late spring – Spring after the Water is Open; cut and stacked hay in summer – Moon Young Ducks Begin to Fly; worked on the threshing gangs in autumn – the Snow Goose Moon; and cut wood and trapped muskrats in the winter and early spring – the Old Moon and Spring Before Open Water. Home was a wagon or rough tent, 8 feet by 12 feet, heated, if at all, by a tin stove.

Whether the Sangrets lived near the white settlers in Battleford or near the Cree reserves of Poundmaker's people, they were likely to have been lumped in the same class by whites as 'fringe' people, drawing phrases from their lips such as 'breeds', 'lazy bums', 'useless misfits' and 'a disgrace to humanity'. Some Métis – known as Hudson Bay Scotch – became relatively successful and affluent, but, rather like the American Negro, this small group only did so by 'crossing the colour line', in other words becoming white in as many respects as possible. The fact that the Sangret family, or at least Napoleon, Sangret's father, was in dire financial straits by 1946, suggests that he was not a successful Métis. The fact that August was constantly unemployed in the 1930s confirms it.

Statistics relating to the Métis are only reliable since the 1950s. The last separate Métis census compiled by the Dominion Bureau of Statistics was held in 1941 when there were only 9,160 of them living in Saskatchewan. D Bruce Sealey and Antoine S Lussier quote some of the information available in 1959, specifically from Manitoba, but they are in fact describing Sangret's childhood in Saskatchewan forty years earlier:

'Many of the homes visited were overcrowded. At Birch River, 15 persons were living in a two-room shack 12' x 24'. There was not enough bedspace for more than six. At Wabowden, a family group of 19 persons lived in three small rooms. A one-room, 14' x 20' long house in another community housed a couple and their seven children. Three small boys slept on the floor, a baby swung from the ceiling in a hammock, the parents slept in a standard double bed and the three teenage girls (the

oldest 18 years old) slept in a smaller bed at the
foot of the parents' bed.'

Schooling for the Métis was very irregular. The whites actively
discouraged them from attending their schools and the schools
on the Indian reserves were usually full. Some ten percent of
Métis lived near reserves, culturally close to their Indian cousins
– the old ways kept alive by frequent contact with them – but
unable to claim the subsistence that 'status' Indians received
from the government. A further ten percent lived in shanty
towns made of scrap timber, tin and cardboard on the edge of
white settlements. 'In a sense,' write Sealey and Lussier, 'they
were a people who had no future and were cheated of the
present because the past was filled with pain, sorrow, hunger
and despair.' Even in 1959, 23 per cent of Métis in Manitoba
had received no education at all and a staggering 69 per cent of
their parents (Sangret's generation) had never been to school.

Not in time for August Sangret, the Métis made some
effort to help themselves, to rekindle in political debate the
pride and élan that had characterised Gabriel Dumont's
horsemen, his hunters of the plains. Too late to recreate the
nation that Louis Riel dreamed of, the Métis of Saskatchewan
formed their first Association in 1937. Twenty years later, the
signs of prejudice were everywhere. The most prejudiced were
those who worked closest with the Métis – their fellow
labourers, their foremen, their employers. Métis men were
hired as a last resort and fired first. And the provincial
government of Saskatchewan did not offer financial support
until 1946.

What did all this amount to in the case of August Sangret,
from Battleford, where, only twenty-eight years before he was
born, Poundmaker's Crees had danced triumphant through the
deserted streets, smashing furniture and stealing provisions? It
amounted to a man used to poverty, to scruffy women like
Joan Wolfe; a man familiar with want and wary of policemen; a
man not likely to confide in whites unless he had to. Above all,
it created – and this is why we have needed to understand the

racial background of the Métis – a man who had essentially given up. 'The first half of the twentieth century,' write Sealey and Lussier, 'did not belong to the Métis ... [their] mental set ... was one of hopelessness.' The same 'mental set' that led August Sangret to say, 'Someone did it. And I guess I will have to take the rap.'

The Métis had been taking the rap for two generations by 1942.

What do we know of the man waiting for death in the condemned cell at Wandsworth Prison? Of his early life, only what he himself tells us, via his court testimony at Kingston Assizes on Friday, 26 February. He was born on 28 August 1913 at Battleford. His parents were French Indians and he was, by religion, a Catholic. He never attended school, in Canada or anywhere else, and could not read or write beyond signing his name. In the papers from the Government Records Branch of the National Archives of Canada (called for convenience here the Sangret papers) his signature is shaky and the letters are ill-formed, as though each one is a real effort for him. You can almost hear the sigh of relief as he crosses the final 't'.

At home he spoke English and a mixed patois – largely Cree and English with 'some words in French'. Asked by Linton Thorp whether he understood English, Sangret said he did 'but there are some big words I cannot understand'. He had been a farm labourer in Maidstone, Saskatchewan and from 1935 to 1939 had served in the Battleford Light Infantry, a militia regiment, which involved two weeks' training a year. On 19 June 1940, Sangret enlisted in the Regina Rifles Regiment.

That is all he was asked for at the trial and, since his early life appeared to have no bearing on the case, Eric Neve did not pursue it in cross-examination. It is one of the peculiarities of the twentieth century that it produces institutions like the armed forces which are all but buried in red tape. So we actually know a great deal more about August Sangret than the jury at his trial did. There are certain days when he was in hospital when we even know his temperature.

Although the Regina Rifles ought to be an infantry unit and Sangret's enlistment in it accords with his four-year militia training, the regiment appears in 1940 to have been part of the Royal Canadian Army Service Corps, that section of the army which traditionally provides transport and related back-up services. His number was L-27572 and it features on most of the documents in the Sangret papers. Among those papers is his attestation (enlistment) form completed on 19 June by Major Sharp at North Battleford. He is listed as single and a labourer engaged in mixed farming. His last employer before service was a Mr Robinson. After the war, Sangret intended to return to the mixed farming he claimed to have done 'all his life'. He was fingerprinted. Under the heading 'Languages' is written 'English and Cree'. Below that Sharp has written, 'No education'.

His next of kin was his father, Napoleon Sangret, who lived in Maidstone. His mother was dead. In another of the Sangret papers, that applying for War Service Gratuity, the rest of the large Sangret family is listed. His father was sixty-one by 1943, his signature as ill-formed as his son's, and he was said to be in desperate financial need. August's eldest brother, David, was thirty-six. A letter written by him, if indeed it is his handwriting, is competent without being over-articulate. Next came Percy – at twenty-three, six years August's junior. Those two lived in Maidstone. Wilfred, a seventeen-year old half brother, lived in Battleford and the other half-brothers, George (fourteen) and Roderick (eleven) lived in Maidstone. Eighteen-year-old half-sister Eva lived at Welland, Ontario and the youngest Sangret child, half-sister Margaret, aged eight, lived in Maidstone.

Sangret's occupational history form says that had had no schooling and no trade apprenticeship. He was unemployed at the time of enlistment, but was employed fairly regularly as a common labourer. His dental records compiled on 15 July 1940 talk of fair oral hygiene, one tooth missing from the left lower jaw and four teeth showing signs of decay. A prophylaxis (i.e. treatment) was recommended, presumably so that serving soldiers should not fall prey to toothache when on active duty. This had been a serious problem in the First World War, when the units in Gallipoli had no dentists with the army at all.

The medical examiners' certificate, again compiled on the day of Sangret's enlistment, is fascinating because it gives the lie to both Joan's and Greeno's descriptions of him. In a letter written to her friend 'Pop' in August, Joan said of Sangret, 'He has black, curly hair, brown eyes, is fairly tall and dark-skinned … and he comes from the West of Canada. He is twenty-eight years old and he is half French and half Indian, but he is ever so nice.' And Greeno remembered, 'He was a handsome brute, stocky … with a deep chest and massive shoulders.'

Sangret was in fact 5 feet 4½ inches tall, virtually the same height as Joan (although he would presumably have appeared taller in his army boots), and his chest measurement, on full expansion, was only 36½ inches, with a 1½ inch range of expansion. On the day of enlistment, he weighed 135 pounds and at his heaviest (in November 1941) was only 147 pounds. Clearly this does not preclude his shattering Joan's skull with a single blow but the huge muscle-bound animal we picture from Greeno and Molly Lefebure vanishes in the face of calm, collected facts. His hearing was 20 feet in both ears. The vision in his right eye was 20/30 and his left 20/20. His intelligence was said to be 'good average' despite his illiteracy. In other words, Sangret was physically A1 and was still in this category when he was last examined in January 1942.

His service record is rather less than admirable. In July 1940 he was transferred with his regiment to Dundurn Camp. On 28 August he was Absent Without Leave for four days and twenty hours, for which he served 120 hours' detention. At the end of September, the Regina Rifles left Dundurn and arrived at Debert Camp, North Saskatchewan on 3 October. On 20 November and again on 4 December, he was AWL again, the first time for one day, fifteen hours, one minute and the second for fifteen hours, two minutes, for which he was admonished (by whom is not recorded). On 5 January 1941, he was given 6 days' special leave, although the official documents give no reason for this. All was quiet until 6 May when Sangret broke out of barracks and was AWL for four days, two hours and fifteen minutes. He served 168 hours' detention. All these abscondings from barracks are the mark of an unhappy man who perhaps could not adjust to army life. We have no explanation as to why he did it or where he went while he was AWL. It set a pattern in Sangret's military life to the extent that slipping out of Camp 103 to sleep with Joan was almost second nature to him. Such activities in wartime were potentially dangerous and may ultimately have led to charges of desertion. There is no record however of Sangret having to be brought back – he simply returned. Perhaps there was some comfort in the King's uniform after all.

On 6 July, just over a year after Sangret had enlisted, his regiment received leave prior to embarkation for Britain. He spent some time, while still at Debert Camp, in Halifax Military Hospital between late July and the end of August. At the end of September, he was up to his old tricks again and forfeited three days' pay for being AWL from 2200 hours to 0305 hours and for 'conduct to the prejudice of good order and Military Discipline in that he was improperly dressed by having his battledress blouse unbuttoned at 0305 hours 27.9.41'. Having had another spell in hospital, Sangret was granted a month's sick leave and given $85 subsistence for that period. By the end of October, the Category A1 soldier was temporarily Category D and the end of November again saw him at the Halifax Military Hospital where he lost fourteen days' pay - $10.50.

On 18 February 1942, Sangret was transferred to the Special Reinforcement (CDIRU) Camp, Sussex. He arrived in England on 24 March and was stationed at Fleet, Hampshire until July. His life pattern continued in this country. On 4 April he lost three days' pay and was confined to barracks for fourteen days for 'conduct to the prejudice of good order and military discipline in that he did use obscene language to an NCO.' For much of April, he was in the 14th Canadian

General Hospital, with the painful condition of conjunctivitis. His eyes were painted with a solution of 1 percent Agno 3. He had been complaining of eye strain since his first week in Britain and he also complained of pains in the chest. On 8 April he was examined and his glands were palpable. He told the medical officer that he had suffered these pains for a year. His father had tuberculosis, he said, a brother was invalided out of the army because of it and a sister had died from it. The X-ray result on the 22nd, however, was negative and the doctors concluded that the pains were muscular.

It is difficult to avoid the conclusion that Sangret was a malingerer, although this is spelt out nowhere in the official records. In one respect, however, his physical complaint was genuine. He had VD.

Sangret's Venereal Case Card, dated three weeks before he met Joan Wolfe and compiled by the Royal Canadian Army Medical Corps at Rushmoor, Aldershot, attempts a case history. His first infection took place in 1931 (Sangret was seventeen), when he treated himself at home, on medical advice, with potassium permanganate solution. This clearly didn't work and he spent thirty-one days in hospital in Battleford because of an obstructed bladder. The 1½ inch scar on his pubis referred to in his enlistment medical report, which he said was the result of an accident in 1934, was in fact a supra-pubic incision to help him urinate. In the Sangret papers all reference to others which might cause offence has been removed. The one exception refers to his first infection. He caught the disease, he claimed, from 'Miss Libby', who was thirty years old, five foot tall, had brown hair, was not attractive, spoke English, was above average weight and worked in and lived above the World's Cafe in Battleford. They'd been drinking at the time and her fee was 50c.

He became infected once more on 15 July 1941 (by which time of course he was in the army), again at Battleford. This time his paramour's details have been blanked out. All we know is that Sangret 'paid no money'.

Again, when Sangret landed in Britain, he brought his lifestyle with him. In May he went on leave, for some reason, to Glasgow, but even in February, he had been admitted to hospital having been 'exposed' six days earlier. The urethritis he complained of may have been a recurrence of the old infection (notoriously difficult to treat in those days) or gonorrhoea as a result of 'sexual exposure' in Glasgow or on 16 June in Fleet. The last encounter involved a 'civilian amateur' and two hours later Sangret had used the standard prophylaxis, Sanitube. He was not drunk at the time. At Rushmoor, Aldershot, a somewhat prudish Canadian army doctor wrote against the infection dates – 'very promiscuous'.

It was the misfortune of both of them that the very promiscuous August Sangret met the equally promiscuous Joan Wolfe.

Between 1938 and 1942 Sangret had no fewer than five admissions to hospitals with venereal disease. Wassermann tests were carried out on him two days after they found Joan's body on Hankley Common. Four days later they proved negative. He was cured.

Many of the Sangret papers concern the accident he had on the night of Thursday, 11 November 1942. By this time, he had been transferred with his unit to Salamanca Barracks, Aldershot. He was coming down some stone steps at half-past eleven at night, missed his footing and fell on his head. No one else was involved, but because it happened on army property, a court of inquiry was conducted on the 24th consisting of three officers, all from the Infantry Reinforcement Unit – Captain White of the Royal Scots, Lieutenant Rae of the Queen's Own Regiment of Canada and Lieutenant Ramsay of the Regina Rifles. The inquiry concluded that the whole thing was just one of those natural hazards of the black-out situation and no blame would accrue to anyone. As for Sangret, he was all right. The blow to the head – traumatic otitis media right' in the medical jargon of the day – may have perforated his ear drum but there was no fracture of the skull. It could have been the cause of disability later.

But for August Sangret, there was to be no 'later'.

What appears nowhere in the Sangret papers – and it perhaps odd that is no space, for example on the attestation form, for this – is that Sangret had a criminal record. It is not the custom of course for this sort of information to be made known prior to a criminal case. Neither does it seem to have been introduced after the jury's findings, presumably because in the situation in which he now found himself – guilty of murder where the law prescribed only one sentence – admission of such evidence was irrelevant. Bearing in mind the violent nature of Sangret's offence, however, it may be highly relevant.

In 1932, at the age of eighteen, he was jailed for six months for a violent assault. Six years later, by this time serving with the Battleford Light Infantry, he was jailed for three months for threatening to shoot a woman in a 'triangle' case. The other convictions were for vagrancy and theft, so typical of the level of desperation to which the 'fringe' Métis were reduced from time to time.

What did his contemporaries make of him? One of the peculiarities of the Sangret case is that *no one* spoke for him at the trial other than his appointed counsel, and since we do not have Linton Thorp's closing arguments to the jury, we cannot know the precise line he took. His commanding officer, Major Gray, who might in different circumstances defended Sangret as 'soldier's friend' was among the witnesses for the prosecution; so was Private Wells who had known Sangret since they were boys back in Battleford.

The only photograph I have ever seen of August Sangret was probably taken in Fleet, and Sangret mentions in his marathon statement to Greeno that he'd had it taken. Presumably, it was the one that Joan carried in her handbag. The face is strong, good-looking. There is much of the handsome Plains Cree people in the flat features, the high cheekbones, the dark hair. Etch in braids on the photograph and there is no reason why August Sangret would look out of place alongside the full-blooded Cree, Poundmaker. Certainly, he looks more Indian than earlier Métis like Louis Riel or even his adjutant Gabriel Dumont.

Molly Lefebure wrote nine years after the event, describing Sangret during that bizarre tea-party in the cells below the Kingston court-room – nine years after the jury had found the man guilty of murder:

> 'Sangret was a strongly built young man of medium height, with his Red Indian blood clearly prominent. Straight features, quite impassive, cold, glittering dark eyes. Straight [sic] dark hair and a red-bronze skin. With an appetite not at all impaired by the ghastly predicament in which he found himself, he enjoyed a large tea, eating and drinking noisily, holding the thick slices of bread and butter with both hands. Not a gracious individual with whom to share a wigwam, I mused. And not likely to make anybody a doting, devoted, baby-dandling husband either. Did he let out a blood-curdling whoop as he crushed Joan's skull in? One could well imagine it.'

Keith Simpson, in *Forty Years of Murder* at least, permits himself no such intuitive luxuries. He makes no moral judgement on Sangret at all, other than to state, as other commentators have, that the jury's recommendation to mercy can as a surprise.

Sangret, as we have seen, was sent to the 3rd Canadian Division Infantry Reinforcement Unit. As such he was in the second wave of Canadian troops sent over here, the first suffering appalling casualties in the abortive raid on Dieppe in August 1942. On 13 July he was posted to the newly formed Educational Company at the 5th Division Infantry Unit. Mr Justice Macnaghten explained the reason for this in his summing up:

'I think it is quite clear that this educational course, instead of being a course in higher education, was a course for men who were lacking in very elementary education. That is why Sangret was sent to this course, not because he knew so much and could be improved by learning more, but because he knew so little that it was thought desirable to bring him and the others upon that course up to something like a normal standard of education.'

Sangret of course wasn't alone in this illiterate predicament.

'I dare say you noticed various other witnesses [and tantalizingly he does not say which ones, although we can assume Private Wells was among them] were called who were also on the educational course and it may have struck you that they did not seem to be men whose education was up to the normal standard prevailing either in this country or in Canada.'

This lack of education in Sangret meant that the love affair with Joan Wolfe *had* to become public. Someone had to read his letters to him. If he wanted to reply, someone had to write his letter for him. What are we to make of his statements to the police?

Conventionally, police statements are taken down in longhand, normally, in capital cases at least, by a detective sergeant, and are a verbatim record of what has been said. There have recently cases in this country in which such statements have clearly been concocted by the police and this has led to a radical rethink of the way in which evidence is collected. We have seen that Sangret's first statement to Greeno (given in October) is one of the longest in criminal history, taking five days for DS Hodge to write it down. Conventionally, too, the statement then has to be read back to its maker and he has to sign it, usually with a sentence in his own handwriting to the effect that 'this has been read to me and is true'. Specifically, Sangret's read, 'This statement has been read over to me and it is true, every bit of it, and I understand it.' It was then signed by him.

It is highly unlikely that Sangret could manage to write anything except his name, although we have no way of knowing what effect twelve weeks with the Educational Company had had on him. Did Greeno have reason to doubt Sangret's ability to understand his own statement? Is that why the phrase 'and I understand it' was included?

At the trial, Linton Thorp quizzed Greeno closely about the exact times when Sangret made his marathon statement. He began, apparently, on 12 October between 2.30 and 3 p.m., and continued until the early hours of the following morning, not talking all the time. For instance, there was a break in the evening, when Sangret took Greeno over to Thursley (actually Kettlebury) to show him 'the old lady's house' where Joan had stayed. From 8.30 p.m. until 3 or 3.30 a.m. the saga continued, punctuated by four breaks of ten minutes each during which quantities of coffee and biscuits were consumed. At that point, Sangret said he was tired and would like a rest. A bed was fixed up for him at Godalming police station and they started again at 10.30 on the morning of Thursday, 13 October. They had a two-hour lunch break, then back to work between 2.30 and 5 p.m., when everything stopped for tea. After that, they went on until 7.30 or 8 in the evening. Again, Sangret slept at the station. Wednesday followed an exactly similar pattern, but Greeno was called away on the Thursday morning and no statement was taken that day. On Friday, they returned to camp by 2.30 p.m.

Linton Thorp asked Greeno if he thought Sangret had spoken quite slowly. 'Did it strike you that he was not particularly familiar with the English language?'

'Yes. He could speak English all right.'

We are bedevilled here by the flat text of the transcript page. Greeno's 'yes' implies that he didn't think Sangret spoke

English very well; his subsequent sentence is ambiguous. Is the detective telling us that Sangret's grasp of spoken English was only adequate? Or is he being ironic, in which case his first answer of 'yes' hardly makes sense. Pursued further by defence counsel, Greeno said that he believed Sangret's statement was slow because 'he was only thinking about what he had been doing.' In *War on the Underworld*, Greeno remembers that 'Sangret had a soft voice and he spoke slowly but he was never lost for words . . .'

Years later, with inevitable hindsight, Superintendent Tom Roberts of the Surrey CID put a different gloss on it: 'Cunning and guile were evident in all his answers, self-preservation was his one objective.'

A rough calculation gives us the fact that Sangret was talking for eighteen and a half hours. In that time, he managed seventeen pages, less than a page an hour. Even for a man trying to remember his movements, even (let's accept Roberts' and the court's verdict) a man trying to lie his way carefully out of a murder charge, that is pitifully slow. Sangret spoke a local patois at home; he could not write anything, so far as we know, other than his name. Was he *really* able to deliver a statement of the type Greeno presented? Presumably he was; or at least, neither Sangret nor his defence counsel seriously challenged it. That they didn't speaks volumes for the limitations either of Sangret's intelligence or of the British judicial system – or of both.

There was of course an additional element to Sangret's illiteracy and it was something commented on by various contemporaries – something perhaps at the very heart of this case. That was his racial origin. There is an aura of disdain in Macdonald Critchley's comment on the Métis in the Canadian forces.

'During the war, racial admixtures often presented disciplinary problems. Especially was this the case when ill-educated, unsophisticated recruits were inducted and then transported abroad, so that they found themselves for the first time masters of such incredible delights as hard liquor [which many authorities believe the Cree had a natural antipathy to and an inability to handle], cash in plenty and complaisant women on all sides. Indian half-breed troops during the war did not lack courage, but they made troublesome and inefficient soldiers, not amenable to discipline and liable to get out of hand during inactive periods of campaigning.'

Much of this had to do with London night-spots, the more lurid eye-catching headlines of the tabloid newspapers and the general readiness of many Britons to lump Americans and Canadians together and to see them almost as 'the enemy'. In fact, taken together, the Canadian Army stationed in this country was well behaved. A report issued in the month that Joan Wolfe died listed 923 who had been convicted in civil courts since December 1939, for a variety of crimes including theft, larceny, burglary and assault. Given the large number over here (nearly 205,000 by December 1943) the ratio is that for every 10,000 Canadians, four or five each month wound up in court. Five men, other than Sangret, were convicted of murder in the six years of the war.

The point was of course that Sangret wasn't just Canadian; he was Métis, a half-breed and his Indian pedigree seemed paramount. It is the sort of racial mistrust – the mere fact that the man was *different* – that led Greeno to describe him as 'a handsome *brute*', and sent a shiver down the spine of Molly Lefebure. Macdonald Critchley goes further.

> 'The French half-breed squatters are known to be proud, sensitive and impulsive. The attack upon Joan Wolfe certainly conforms with what we might expect of a sullen, untutored half-breed, goaded into fury.'

And Greeno quotes an anonymous Canadian brigadier, presumably from Witley Camp, who described his Métis as 'good men, good fighters. Sometimes a bit sullen though and sometimes with a streak of the real savage ...' Greeno admitted to looking for that streak in Sangret, perhaps a little over-zealously.

In adopting this slightly disapproving, slightly awestruck attitude, all four are following the line of men who worked with Sangret. Sergeant Charles Hicks, of the Toronto Scottish, who had the probably unenviable task of doing something about the man's illiteracy, said that Sangret was 'a very quiet man in class and did not appear to hold much conversation with anybody.' At the trial, Linton Thorp asked him if Sangret was upset when he discovered, via a letter from Joan, which Hicks read to him, that she was pregnant.

'No, he was not,' Hicks remembered. 'None of these chaps are usually. What I mean is that it takes a lot to upset an Indian chap.'

Either Hicks or the official records are at fault, because the sergeant believed that Sangret reached Witley camps between 6 and 9 July; the Sangret papers say the 13th. It is also curious that Hicks said at the trial that he regarded Sangret as an Indian, 'having seem the particulars in his paybook.' While conceding that the man was 'half French and half Indian', that didn't seem to make much difference. D. Bruce Sealey and Antoine S. Lussier make the same comment. In the eyes of many white Canadians, there *was* no distinction between the Métis and the Indian.

Sergeant Harold Wade, who had been so solicitous over Joan's welfare, also found Sangret unfathomable. Asked by the prosecution whether the Métis seemed worried about Joan's disappearance, he said '... that is a hard question to answer because he is the type of man with what we call a poker face and it is hard to say just what is going on in his mind.'

And what of Joan Wolfe, the woman who loved him? Her testimony is like an echo down the years, enshrined for ever on scraps of paper and on the worn timbers of an old cricket pavilion.

> 'Gosh, darling, I was never ill when you looked after me … we have had some good laughs, and tears too … When I turned over I missed you putting your arms around me … We have always been together until now. The old fire in the evenings and the blackberries and heaps of little things we used to do … I keep smiling for soon we will be together for always … because I love you more than anything else in the world.'

No doubt she did. And no doubt she saw him through the rose-tint of a desperately lonely girl who gave herself fully and freely – and often. Weeks earlier she may have written a similar letter to Francis Hearn, the Canadian she had been due to marry at Godalming.

To her friend 'Pop' she wrote, '… he is half French and half Indian, but he is ever so nice.' What kind of deep, subconscious racism, I wonder, is lurking in that typically English 'but'?

Though there were no character witnesses at Sangret's trial and no defence witnesses other than himself, the Canadian authorities kept a paternal, if distant, eye on him. Men like Gray and Wade, and indeed the local police, seem to have been tolerant, in some ways indulgent towards Sangret, but I believe that this was for Joan's sake. People who knew her spoke of her charm, her sweetness – for all her rough living and questionable morals, her *innocence*. Some of them, no doubt, had daughters Joan's age. All of them were aware of the effect that war was having on young, half-formed lives. So when Wade and Hicks and Gray talked to Sangret of marriage, I believe it was to try to solve her problems, not his.

The war diary of Captain F B Creasey, the Deputy Assistant Provost-Marshal, Canadian Reinforcements Units, contains a number of entries relating to the case. On 14 October he went to Godalming and met Chief Inspector Greeno, 're the body of woman found in Thursley area'. Sangret of course was in the process of delivering his epic statement at this time and it is not recorded whether he actually spoke to Sangret. By the 30th, the DAPM was aware of a hardening in police attitudes. This time, Greeno and Superintendent Webb came to him 're murder of Joan Pearl Wolfe ... Pte Sangret, A 3 CIDRU, Suspect.'

On 11 December, the DAPM went to Guildford 'to attend trial [hearing at the magistrates' court] of Pte August Sangret ... charged with the murder of Joan Pearl Wolfe ... remanded to 1 Jan '43.'

The next entries refer to the start of the New Year and Brixton Prison. This was one of the London gaols, along with Wandsworth, which was built to replace the inadequate medieval institutions of Southwark. Rising out of designs first promulgated in 1819, what should have been a marked improvement on earlier buildings ended up as an overcrowded slum. It was – and is – the principal remand prison for a huge area extending to St Albans in the north, Southend in the east and Guildford to the south. Its entrance is plain and, were it not for a windmill nearby, difficult to locate. In the war years, Brixton held conscientious objectors or those – like Oswald Mosley, the leader of the British Fascists – who had sympathy with the enemy. Regulation 18B and the Defence of the Realm Act kept them there under close supervision. For a while the cell holding Josef Jakobs, a German officer awaiting court martial on charges of espionage, was under military authority.

Sangret requested on 5 January that he had a Catholic chaplain contact. This was confirmed by a phone call on the 7th. On the 9th, Lieutenant Gillis of the Provost-Marshal's Headquarters in London arranged for various witnesses to attend the preliminary hearings at Guildford on 12, 13, 19 and 20 January. Twenty-one members of the Canadian Army appeared – minus Privates Wells and Crowle who were not called to give evidence in the lower court. For whatever reason,

Lance-Corporal Naugler, a military policeman with the Cape Breton Highlanders, did not give evidence in the trial at Kingston.

The only officer among them was Major Talmage Gray of the Canadian Educational Company, referred to in the trial transcript as Sangret's commanding officer. But herein lay a fundamental problem. Although technically, for all everyday purposes, that *was* Gray's role, with hundreds of men passing briefly through his hands, he couldn't possibly have known Sangret well enough to constitute a company commander in the accepted sense. Gray's evidence at the trial (and he was of course yet another prosecution witness) was very matter of fact. He had interviewed Sangret twice, once on 24 August and again on 10 October, both times in connection with Sangret's plans to marry Joan. His evidence is totally unhelpful.

Committal proceedings were completed on 20 January. Interestingly, Captain Creasey's diary entry for that day reads, 'medium strong circumstantial case only'. He notes that Laurence Vine had been briefed at the hearing, but he applied to the Bench for authorization of a second (and, as it turned out, leading) counsel – Linton Thorp. Presumably, both men appeared under the Poor Persons' Defence Act, as the Canadian Army 'has not the facilities for supplying defence counsel'.

Captain Creasey attended the trial but, unless he was called as a material or character witness (neither of which would have been appropriate), all he could do was observe. A BBC researcher looking into the case some years ago refers to a Captain James Johnson 'who stood by him', and states that this man was Sangret's commanding officer. He may have held that post in the Regina Rifles Regiment, but his name appears nowhere in the papers I have read.

On 24 March, Major Nicholson, the Chief Constable of Surrey, wrote an official letter of thanks to Major-General P J Montague of the Canadian Headquarters staff for the help of the Canadians 'in the course of difficult and prolonged investigations which eventually led to the arrest of Sangret.'

What else could the authorities have done? The answer is very little. It may be, of course, from the comment 'medium strong circumstantial only' that the DAPM's office at least expected Sangret to get off. The point was, however, that the authorities' hands were tied. Because they had. At the start of the war, handed cases involving treason, murder, manslaughter, treason-felony and rape over to the civil authority of the British courts, it was not possible for anyone in the Provost-Marshal's department to interfere. And Mr Justice Macnaghten was at pains to point out that the justice Sangret received was identical with that in Canada: '… if this case was being tried in the Province of Saskatchewan as it is joined here, between our Sovereign Lord the King and the prisoner at the Bar and there, as here, a jury of twelve would be empanelled to try the truth of that issue.'

The Court of Criminal Appeal was established in 1907, the year they stopped raising the black flag over prisons as proof that an execution had been carried out. It was in a way a 'court of last resort'. For capital cases, where a man's life was in the balance, it was *de rigeur*. But winning an appeal was not easy. The only grounds on which such a slim victory could occur were if the original trial could be proved to have been mishandled, especially by the judge in his summing up. Even so, this was by no means cast iron. The appeal was held before three judges; colleagues certainly, friends possibly, of the judge charged with incompetence or partiality. The notorious case of Lord Chief Justice Goddard, with his five-line 'mention' of the case for Derek Bentley in a summing up running to several pages in 1952, is testimony of what the appellant was up against. There could be no retrial, even in the light of new evidence.

Mr Justice Macnaghten's summing up and charge to the jury had been exemplary. It seemed that the appeal in this case just consisted of everyone concerned going through the motions. Greeno calls it a farce. Perhaps Captain Creasey, the DAPM, or Captain White, Adjutant of the Regina Rifles, suggested that Sangret lodge the appeal. At any rate, he handed in his own notice rather than the more usual pattern of his defence counsel doing so.

On Tuesday, 13 April, before Viscount Caldecote, the Lord Chied Justice, Mr Justice Humphries and Mr Justice Lewis, the appeal was heard. The fierce-looking Thomas Inskip, 1st Viscount Caldecote was called to the Bar in 1897 and took silk at the start of the Great war. In 1918 he was head of the naval law branch of the Admiralty. Knighted in 1922, he represented Bristol Central as Conservative MP throughout the '20s and had a highly distinguished career in the law after that. He was twice Attorney-General, three times Solicitor-General and Minister for the hastily convened Co-ordination of Defence in the run-up to the Second World War. Interestingly for the Sangret case, he was briefly Dominions Secretary before being elevated to the Lords as Lord Chancellor in 1940. Between that year and 1946, the year before his death, he was Lord Chief Justice.

As was customary, the original counsel, prosecution and defence were present, but as the motion for appeal had come from the accused, there was really nothing Linton Thorp could say on its behalf. He had been through the summing up again and again, but there was 'no complaint that could be made with regard either to it or to the conduct of the trial'. It was simply that the jury, after a perfectly proper summing up, had chosen not to find Sangret innocent. They had, in the official transcript's words, 'disbelieved the story told by the appellant.' Linton Thorp reminded their lordships however of the jury's strong recommendation to mercy. It was a pity that nobody remembered that Greeno had kept Sangret for five days without charging him. Well, there *was* a war on …

Caldecote made his ruling. The only question in the case was whether the jury had decided on the evidence before them that Sangret was Joan's killer. The evidence of their liaison, between the middle of July and the middle of September, was irrefutable. They lived together in two different shacks at different times, as well as at the cricket pavilion. There had been proper direction by the judge and 'an abundance of evidence of a circumstantial character pointing to the fact that the appellant was the murderer of the girl.' There was no point of law to quibble over and 'no possible ground on which the verdict could be disturbed.' As for the recommendation to mercy, that was not a matter for the Court of Appeal. That was lodged with the Home Secretary.

'The man who rations mercy' at that time was Herbert Morrison. He had been born in Brixton, within a stone's throw of the prison, and was merely a toddler when the Ripper struck terror to the East End. With an elementary school education and jobs as errand-boy, shop assistant, telephone operator and deputy circulation manager of a newspaper, he did not, at first glance, have the necessary credentials for a cabinet post. Through joining the Labour Party and holding various local government posts in the London County Council, however, he entered the Commons as MP for South Hackney in 1923. At first, in Churchill's coalition government, he was Minister of Supply, but in October 1940 became Home Secretary. I am aware of no correspondence relating to Morrison's decision. Perhaps, like Keith Simpson, Molly Lefebure and policemen various, he found the jury's recommendation to mercy a surprise, or even inexplicable. This was not a controversial case in the full glare of peacetime publicity. A man had been found guilty, by a legally constituted court, of murder. There was only one sentence. The death penalty. Let the law take its course.

August Sangret spent the last days of his life in the tiny condemned cell at Wandsworth Prison. On the other side of the sliding metal wall from him was the apparatus of death – a trapdoor, a frame and a lever. How aware he was of its close proximity we shall never know. Wandsworth was one of those 'model' prisons of which the Victorians were so proud, opened in 1865. By the early years of this century, it had become a hanging prison, and never more so than during the years of the war. Refugees arriving from Nazi-occupied Europe were marshalled at the Royal Victoria Patriotic School, which stood across the road from the prison. Some of these were tried with the greatest speed and secrecy and executed at Wandsworth. In 1994 the scaffold was dismantled and the condemned suite is now used as an officers' tea room.

Here, through March and April of 1943, August Sangret waited to meet his fate.

8

Who Killed the Wigwam Girl?

At shortly after 2.55 p.m. on the afternoon of Tuesday, 1 March 1943, twelve anonymous members of the British public – 'good men and true' – decided that the answer to the question posed above was: August Sangret. The judge, Mr Justice Macnaghten, did not disagree. Neither did the three judges of the Appeal Court. The Canadian Army authorities made no protest. They merely noted down on their official documents that their appeal number 1067 had failed. The Home Secretary, Herbert Morrison, saw no reason to interfere with the due process of the law.

Mr Justice Macnaghten had said in his summing up:

> 'That the girl was murdered is not in dispute; that she was murdered by some man is also quite plain; and the only question you have to determine is: Have the Crown satisfied you beyond all real doubt that the prisoner, August Sangret, is the man who murdered her?'

He reiterated the point at the end:

> 'I can only conclude by saying what I said at the beginning: when dealing with a case of circumstantial evidence you must be satisfied beyond all doubt before you find the prisoner is guilty. If you come to the conclusion that, on

the facts proved to you, no real doubt is left in your minds that his was the hand which slew this unhappy girl, then you will convict him.'

J.H.H Gauté and Robin Odell in their masterly *Murder What Dunnit* define circumstantial evidence as evidence which 'is derived from facts not in dispute from which can be inferred a fact that is at issue' and they cite the example of Robinson Crusoe's finding a footprint in the sand from which he inferred there was a stranger on the island. Fine: but what Crusoe was not entitled to do was to infer that the footprint belonged to Man Friday. Nor can we blithely assume, as the jury did, that the murderous knife with the parrot's beak and the equally murderous birch stake were wielded by August Sangret.

Gauté and Odell rightly point out that circumstantial evidence 'has acquired a bad name and is popularly regarded as unreliable and inferior to direct evidence or eyewitness testimony. The fact is of course that there is rarely an eyewitness to murder, especially if the crime is premeditated. On that basis, circumstantial evidence is used commonly in law courts.'

Not for the first or last time, the ass that is the law does not share the public's commonsense point of view, and regularly upholds circumstantial evidence – presumably on the vague lines expressed by criminologist F Tennyson Jesse who has argued that, while 'they can be misinterpreted, circumstances themselves do not lie.'

Gauté and Odell cite the case of Professor John Webster, tried in 1850 for the murder of a colleague, Dr George Parkman, known to his Harvard students as 'the Chin' because of his pronounced lower jaw. Chief Justice Lemuel Shaw said:

> 'Experience has shown that circumstantial evidence may be offered in such a case; that is a body of facts may be proved of so conclusive a character as to warrant a firm belief of the fact quite as strong and certain as that on which

discreet men are accustomed to act in relation
to their most important concerns...'

It is extraordinary that this case, notoriously corrupt in the way
it was handled, should have established such a shaky precept
that, astonishingly, it not only stood the test of time in
American law, but became enshrined in British law too. Such
was the rowdiness of the Bostonians who watched the Webster
trial that the judge kept clearing the courtroom. It was
estimated that an amazing 55,000 people had eventually
witnessed bits of it. One of the expert witnesses, the dentist Dr
Nathan Keep, was a personal friend of the dead man and his
moving performance in the witness box had the entire jury in
tears. Such a partisan piece of trickery was bizarre even in 1850
and would certainly not be tolerated today. In that Webster
confessed to his crime, the judge's comments in this instance
seem to have been borne out. But Sangret did not confess to
his and we are left with a different set of conclusions.

Who, then, killed Joan Wolfe? The answer, in a case
involving circumstantial evidence, is that almost anyone *could*
have done. There were 100,000 soldiers in the area of the
Witley and Thursley camps between the summer and Christmas
of 1942, not to mention an unspecified number of civilian
locals and not even considering the imponderable number of
civilian strangers who might have been in the area. Greeno and
Webb felt that their case was secure; so, obviously, did the
Director of Public Prosecutions, counsel for the prosecution
and, ultimately, jury and judge. The fact is, however, that there
were gaps in the prosecution case which have never been
satisfactorily plugged. All subsequent writers on the Wigwam
Murder have relished the grisly aspects of the case and looked
upon it (rightly) as a triumph of forensic science and detection.
'This was nearly', says Greeno, 'the perfect crime – a murder
not only unsolved, but undiscovered.' The only writer to
examine seriously the emotional tangle behind the murder is
Macdonald Critchley in the *Notable British Trials* series, and
arguably his slant is wrong.

What was the circumstantial case against Sangret? The evidence of his statement – the marathon effort dictated over five days, which Webb found so incriminating and which Greeno did not – is worthy of careful reconsideration. He met Joan Wolfe on 17 July in a public house opposite the cinema. There were only two or three others there, all of them Canadian soldiers, and Sangret was on his second pint when the girl arrived. He said 'Good evening,' to her and offered to buy her a drink. She stuck to her lemonade. In the course of their conversation, she mentioned a boy named Francis who had been about to marry her, but he had been sent back home on the previous Thursday. They walked in the park and beyond the railway station and he made love to her – 'I did not use a French letter and I just did it the natural way.' They met again outside the fish and chip shop on the 21st when the police constable had come along and taken Joan to the station. Afterwards, she returned to the grassland just before midnight and made love again. She stood him up the next night and it was not until the following Friday that he received her first letter, from the Warren Road Hospital in Guildford. Sergeant Hicks wrote a reply for him, but Sangret mistimed the visiting hours on the Sunday and couldn't see Joan. Private Hartnell wrote another letter explaining all this.

Late July was a series of near misses. Joan called at the camp on 29th, but Sangret was watching a show at the camp and the soldiers she sent to locate him couldn't find him.

On the 30th, while he was at a class, she sent a message to say she was waiting outside. The ever-tolerant Sergeant Hicks let him out to see her and they discussed the contents of her second letter to him, that she was pregnant. 'Joan … had called to see me and to tell me she was in the family way. Joan began talking about getting married and I told her I would marry her.'

That night he built the first of the wigwams for her behind the officers' lines. 'Joan told me she had nowhere to live, so I built a small shack from branches of trees, put my rain cape, and my gas cape over the branches and then covered this with leaves and twigs.' He took his blankets, answered roll call at ten and slipped out to sleep with her. He described her appearance to Greeno in vivid detail.

> 'Joan took off her coat which was a long, light brown one, I don't remember whether it had any pockets in it, it had no belt, was tight waisted, had black buttons and a small collar. She carried a black shiny leather handbag, about nine inches long [this was never found] six inches high and two inches thick. It had two white metal knobs on the top where it fastened … It contained a bunch of pictures, there was one of myself *and of other soldiers* [my italics] … also a picture of her father, all I think of postcard size. The picture I gave her I had taken in Fleet. I gave the man my name and number and it was sent on to me at the camp.'

He describes in astonishing clarity Joan's comb, her lipstick, her powder compact and her Bible: 'I also saw in her handbag, a small cross with a figure of Jesus on it. The cross was very thing, I believe it was black on the front and tin colour on the other side.'

Her clothes too were indelibly imprinted on his extraordinary memory.

> 'She also wore a greenish coloured dress, with some white in it, and it had a white collar with fancy work around the edge. It had short sleeves. It was a long dress and she wore a shiny black belt with a buckle on it … She wore underneath her dress a sort of silky shirt with shoulder straps. It had no sleeves. She also wore something to hold her breasts up. I don't know what you call them. Underneath she wore short silky knickers, I think they had some fancy work or lace on parts of them. She used to take them

off when I had connexions with her. She did not wear stockings but small socks with blue and red rings round them. Her shoes were dark in colour and they had laces in them. Joan told me she bought them for 5s at a second hand shop in Godalming. They were low-heeled shoes. The laces were a kind of cord and were different in colour to the shoes. The shoes had no toe-caps and were second hand. Joan did not wear a hat but had a small handkerchief, I think it was white and pink, over her head and tied under her chin.

'Joan wore a wedding ring on one of the fingers of her left hand. I think it was gold and about an eighth of an inch wide … I should say she was round about five feet tall, stout build, fair complexion, small slim face, bluey grey eyes, fair hair cut short like a boy with a parting at the side. As for as I can remember her teeth were a little dark coloured and were fairly good teeth. Her fingernails were round and not painted.'

What are we to make of this incredible detail? Greeno could have asked for no finer witness in terms of recall. He may even secretly have regretted that Sangret was not at the Yard! In *War on the Underworld*, he says '… his memory was phenomenal. He could remember dates and fit the days to them and when we checked the calendar, he was always right.'

When I began to research for this book, it was in the belief that Sangret was very limited in terms of intelligence, that he could not adequately defend himself in a court of law or against the police because his intellect was not up to it. After talking to the Bonners, who met him as children, I realized that this was not the impression he gave to casual passers-by: although children can be wrong and 1942 is a long time ago for the memory to cope with, no one makes the point that Sangret was anything other than normal. He was uncouth, he was illiterate, he was a loner, but that does not help us decide on his IQ.

This section of his statement suggests two things. First, the importance to an illiterate man of the spoken word. His Cree background made this vital. The Cree had no written alphabet. They had an oral and sign language tradition with which all their memories and all their history was conveyed. Sangret could not go away and look things up in books. He carried it all around in his head. Second, we may nevertheless have here an example of the idiot savant, a man of child-like qualities, of naivety and innocence, who has an extraordinary ability in one tiny field – in this case an amazing eye for detail and recall of material facts. There is a third possibility, suggested to me by Mrs Carolyn Smith, then Educational Psychologist with the Isle of Wight Education Authority. Without knowing who Sangret was and of what he stood accused, Mrs Smith came to the (necessarily guarded) conclusion that he may have been unable to register emotions or even understand them. This would accord with contemporaries' descriptions of his 'poker face' and 'you never know with Indian chaps'.

The pair met regularly in the first week of August at Milford Crossroads, went for a walk in the balmy summer evening and back to the shack by nine. 'There were some gloriously hot days in August 1942,' Greeno remembered, 'and some passionately hot nights.' Sangret answered roll call, then joined his lover and 'had connexions' (Greeno's phrase? Hodges'?) every night. It was in this period that Joan lied to Sangret, claiming that she was working in the balloon factory canteen. In fact, he discovered she had lost her job through coming in late after the first two or three days.

Sleeping rough was a problem. Sangret was concerned that she would catch cold and that he would be caught AWL (remember that his track record was poor on this score). Joan disappeared for four or five days, visiting London, but had been unable to find a job and came drifting back to the wigwam. The routine continued as before with Sangret sneaking back into camp at six in the morning. The fact that he did this for at least a fortnight says either a great deal for his Cree survival skills or nothing at all for security at Witley Camp. On the fifth night, however, 'one of the Provost policemen, I believe his name is Lebrett' (sic) discovered them in the wigwam and they had to move on. Sangret built a second shack as before with his issue jack-knife and tied the saplings down with parcel string he had 'lifted' from the camp. This second 'home' was about 15-20 yards from the physical training ground and half a mile from the first. Sangret makes it clear that their wanderings around Witley village were little short of begging jaunts – 'I went to a house in the main road nearby and was given a piece of bread.'

It was now that two children, 'about nine or ten years old, both girls' (Rita Bonner and Grace White), helped them look for a room in the village. There was nothing available and they returned to the shack. On the way, Sangret stopped off at a tea shop and, in hurrying to catch her up, realized that Joan was not at the wigwam. He had seen the Provosts nosing around and put two and two together. She was in the guardroom and he was locked up for 'keeping a girl about the camp'. The civilian police arrived and Joan told them she and Sangret intended to marry.

The following day, Sangret was told at Godalming police station that Joan was back at the Warren Road Hospital. A civilian phoned the hospital for him from the kiosk at the top of the hill, near the theatre (cinema). He at lat got to visit her on Saturday, 29 August in the casualty ward and Joan now told him that the doctors were unsure whether she was pregnant. She complained about the hospital and lack of food. By this time, Major Gray was making arrangements for the marriage and had given Sangret £1 to help find lodgings for Joan. The matron allowed Sangret to visit the following Wednesday, but on the previous day, Joan turned up at the camp with her pass valid until eight o'clock. They walked around Godalming, 'had connexions' and ate at the YMCA before he left her at the station – as he thought, to return to the hospital.

It was the next day, the day he had been due to visit Joan at Warren Road, that he saw her sitting by the camp gate as he set out on a route march. She was still thee three hours later. Now Joan decided to try for a room at Kate Hayter's in Thursley, where she had stayed before. Sangret got pies and tea from the NAAFI – his account to Greeno was another extraordinary catalogue of minutiae:

> 'I got the tea in my water-bottle. It is my issue water-bottle given to me in Canada. It is covered with khaki cloth and it is on straps which bear my regimental number. The water-bottle is not marked with my number. I used to carry it in a bag. The bag has two tapes at the top which you pull to fasten. It has two pockets. It is kind of cloth covered. The bag is about eight inches square and was given to me at a hospital in Halifax, Canada.'

He remembered bringing bottles of lemonade for Joan from the NAAFI and she took to drinking it from his water-bottle. She also carried it empty so that she could fill it with tea from the Salvation Army hostel in Godalming. She never used a cup.

They found the house of the old lady, Kate Hayter, on Kettlebury Hill in the dark. Sangret had not been there before, and Joan would not let him come with her to the door. Later, he knew why. As far as the old lady knew, Joan was already married to another Canadian soldier. They drew a blank there and Sangret took Joan that night to an empty house, the floors of which were strewn with papers. He had noticed the place on a route march. Once again, in the police jargon of the time, they 'had connexions'. This 'house' must in fact have been the Thursley cricket pavilion, as it took Sangret an hour to walk from there it Witley Camp. Kate Hayter could still not provide a room – her sister was staying with her – but the situation would ease a week later.

The last days of Joan Wolfe were spent on that bare ridge with the cricket pavilion's back to the tree-lined slopes of Dye House Hill, and Thursley Common stretching to the north-east. 'She did not mind being there alone,' Sangret recalled in his statement. 'She was not a nervous girl.' The old routine developed – Sangret meeting her there at seven, bringing food from the NAAFI, eating with Joan and then reporting for roll call at ten before doubling back to the 'shed' again. He remembered her clothes, the same as when he had first met her, except for a coat someone had given her at the Warren Road Hospital. It was grey check, loose fitting, with no belt or collar. On Sunday, the last day anyone saw her alive, Joan and Sangret hung around the pavilion in the morning, then walked to the place where the tanks trained before he returned to camp for lunch. In the afternoon, they went blackberrying round the crossroads. On Monday morning, 14 September, he left her as usual, at the pavilion at seven o'clock. By this time, the old lady's sister should have left and Joan was to go and see her to try again for a room.

It was that morning that they had a row. Sangret told Joan that he intended to spend his forthcoming leave with Mrs Pattigan, the lady he'd met earlier in Glasgow. Joan was pressing him about their wedding and sensed perhaps that Sangret didn't seem as keen as he had been. She said, 'I don't think you would care to marry me.' 'If I didn't want to marry you,' Sangret replied, 'I should not have lived with you as I have been.' She was crying. The girl had written on Sangret's behalf to Mrs Oak to thank her for the parcels she'd sent him. Despite Sangret's protestations that Mrs Oak was just a friend, Joan told him, 'You can't love two.' Sangret promised not to contact the lady from Glasgow again, but Joan was still furious when they parted, never to meet again. It was their first and last row. 'Goodbye,' she sobbed. 'This is the last time I might see you.'

To get to Kettlebury Hill, Joan would have taken a short cut on the high ridge that runs parallel to the one on which the pavilion stood, the one through Houndown Wood. It was here, perhaps on that Monday morning, that she met her killer.

As we have seen, when Sangret returned that evening (pay day), Private Joseph Wells joined him on the road. Joan was not there. She was still not there when they returned at nine. Sangret's Canadian Army issue knife, with its tin handle and iron spike, was gone, as was his water-bottle. Both these items were lying on the pavilion floor when he saw them last, covered with paper as was his custom. With the extraordinary clarity of vision and obsession with detail which characterise Sangret's statement to the police, he described the size and colour of the tins of paste Joan bought from the village shop.

Here ends Sangret's first statement to Greeno, although the last three pages consist of his remembering odds and ends and repeating phrases, obviously at Greeno's or Hodge's prompting, presumably in an attempt to catch him out. Apart from the catalogue of meetings and the rather sad love story which emerges, there was nothing here which Greeno could use to hold his man, much less arrest him. As Greeno would write years later, the statement boiled down to '… boy meets girl, true love runs unsmooth and suddenly girl disappears, leaving boy sorrowing.'

In response to what clearly were questions, Sangret told the Yard men that he had washed his battledress in ordinary laundry soap, and that he had seen Joan in conversation with at least two other soldiers and didn't approve of the fact; above all, he admitted the row on the last morning of Joan's life. Odd confessions for a guilty man to make, when he had absolutely no need to do so.

Sangret's second statement, Exhibit 45 at his trial, was made on 6 December, after he had enjoyed his leave in Glasgow and while he was still at the Salamanca Barracks. This time Greeno kept Sangret on the move, taking him to Thursley to visit scenes of the lovers' life together. As such, it is a fraction of the length of the first one. Sangret showed Greeno the loop the pair used to walk from the cricket pavilion to the old lady's house on Kettlebury Hill and back again. He showed him the 'creek' where he collected water for their use at the pavilion and the road near Camp 103 where they used to pick blackberries. He showed him the houses on whose doors they had knocked looking for rooms and the road that Sangret took back to his own camp from Thursley. And he showed him the spot where the tanks used to train on the edge of Hankley Common.

The rest of the statement refers to discussions about Sangret's knife. It was read to him by DS Hodge and Sangret signed it with his uncertain, ill-formed signature.

Later that afternoon, Superintendent Webb charged Sangret with the murder of Joan Wolfe.

'No, sir,' the man-in-the-frame had insisted. 'I did not do it, no, sir. Someone did it and I will have to take the rap.'

There is nothing in either of these statements which can point to Sangret as a murderer. Of the three classic elements in murder – motive, means and opportunity – only the last is present. Sangret said he said goodbye to Joan on the morning of Monday, 14 September, an indication that he was with her hours, or even minutes, before she died. He said of course that he left her at the pavilion, over half a mile away from where her body was found and from which Greeno and Simpson had deduced she had been killed. The inability of Simpson or Gardner to pinpoint the exact time of death was a weakness in the prosecution case, because it gave Sangret at least the ghost of an alibi. If Joan died during the day on Monday the 14th, then he could claim to be elsewhere, at class at Jasper Camp or on a route march. The fact that no one saw Joan after Sunday, 13 September does not, of itself, mean that she died that Monday morning. She may even have been alive while Sangret was searching for her.

Greeno believed that Sangret was lying because his version of where the pair were living up to 14 September does not accord with that of Featherby, the ARP warden who said at the trial, and presumably earlier in response to police questioning, that he had moved them on after 9 September. Why should Featherby lie about this? Perhaps because he had softened and let the bedraggled girl stay there after all, and could not admit this to the authorities because of his position. Why should Sangret lie about it? Perhaps so that he could physically distance the pair from Houndown Wood, where he may have built a third wigwam after 9 September. But if he did that, why didn't Webb's sixty coppers, combing the whole area elbow to elbow, come across any sign of it?

But it was not, of course, Sangret's statement that led to his being found guilty. It established opportunity. What the prosecution needed was the means – and that meant linking Sangret with the weapons involved. The forensic evidence of the case, proffered by Simpson, Gardner and Roche Lynch, was a brilliant piece of detective work, surpassing anything produced by Greeno and Webb. And there was no doubt that, however hard Linton Thorp might try to shake them at the trial, the doctors' findings were correct. Joan had been hit by a hook-bladed knife which had punctured her forehead. The same knife had ripped the tendons from her forearm as she instinctively tried to cover her head. She had then run away, bleeding and in agony, scattering the contents of her handbag as she fled, before a single, powerful blow from a birch stake demolished the back of her skull and, where it was crushed against the ground, her right cheekbone. Both weapons had been found.

There is no mention in all the clever forensics of fingerprints. The whorl and loop patterns at the ends of a man's fingers had been carefully noted in Britain by Francis Galton and in Argentina by Juan Vucetich, but it wasn't until Edward Henry became Assistant Commissioner at the Yard in 1901 that anyone took their researches seriously. It was only thirty-seven years before the Wigwam Murder that a case was found against two burglars, the Stratton brothers, solely on the evidence of fingerprints. In the case of Joan Wolfe, in the *absence* of fingerprints, clearly *anyone* could have wielded the stake. The stake itself had been sharpened at both ends, implying that it had been worked. The jury had already heard much of Sangret's wigwams and the method of constructing them. No doubt the assumption was made at the time, as it has been since, that this was part of just such a wigwam that Sangret had made for Joan. There is no evidence, however, that the pair ever lived, even for one night, in Houndown Wood where the police and pathologists believed that Joan died. On the contrary, the two wigwams they built were near the officers' and sergeants' lines on Witley Common, the other side of Thursley and the main London-Portsmouth road, nearly an hour's walk away.

But it was the knife that was more damning. With the exception of that blade tip, of course, it was a conventional British Army knife, no different from thousands of others issued to troops during the war. The fact that it was not *Canadian* issue, however, caused a problem for the prosecution and was one of those holes in the case that was never satisfactorily plugged. Canadian Army knives had tin handles, of metallic colour, and a spike at the back of the blade. The murder weapon had two blades, like the Canadian version, a folding or jack-knife, and had a cross-hatched black horn grip with a metal hanging loop. Confusion crept into the court proceedings when it became apparent that there were two knives – Joan's and Sangret's. Let us look at the wanderings of the tell-tale knife again.

Private Samuel Crowle of the Westminster Regiment had seen the knife that was Exhibit 4 at the trial while blackberrying some time between 12 and 15 August. On the first day he had come across a 'little pile of brush' and a shack with 'some people talking inside' (presumably Sangret and Joan). The next day, on the same errand behind officers' lines at Camp 103, he found the knife. It was, he recalled, 'just stuck in the limb of a tree about 4 feet from the ground and just above the shack'. He knew it was the same knife by 'the nick right in front'. He showed it to the boys blackberrying with him, because this was unlike any knife he had seen. Crowle told his friends he intended to keep it, but one of the Provosts, Corporal Starratt said, 'You have better turn it over to me and I will return it to its owner.' It is from the position of the knife sticking into the tree that Macdonald Critchley infers that Sangret was something of a knife thrower. Clasp knives of this type *can* be thrown, but that is not their purpose and their balance is wrong. It is equally likely that either Sangret or Joan embedded the knife in the tree rather than threw it. Presumably, Crowle recognized the knife in court as the one he had handled because the 'parrot's beak' point would have made it difficult to pull it out of the wood. From the photograph at least the misshapen point is not the most obvious thing about the knife.

From Crowle, the knife passed on 24 August to Lance-Corporal Starratt of the Perth Regiment, then an MP attached to Jasper Camp. What is curious about this testimony is that Crowle implied that Starratt was with him when he found the knife, yet at least nine days had elapsed between Crowle finding it and Starratt's taking possession of it. Unlike Crowle, Starratt had seen such a knife before. He knew that pattern had been issued to British troops stationed at Bordon Camp to the south of Hindhead. The fact, elicited at the trial, was that Starratt did not open the knife. He did not see the blade. We have no way of knowing whether this was the same weapon at all. He left it on the table of Corporal Harding in the guard room at Jasper Camp. He was unsure whether Harding had been there at the time, but he certainly told him about it later the same day.

Corporal Thomas Harding of the Perth Regiment was in charge of the guard room, a photograph of which appeared at the trial but is now lost to time. Harding confirmed that Starratt had given him the knife on that Monday morning, 24 August, and he had put it in a box on the desk. There were no other knives there at that time. Under cross-examination by Linton Thorp, Harding said that he had opened the knife before putting it in the box. He too had seen similar knives 'hanging on the belts of English soldiers', but this one had a 'hooked point on it'. According to Harding, Starratt had told him it was Sangret's knife and Harding had accepted that. He intended to return it to him that day, but in the event didn't until the Wednesday (26 August), when Sangret came in to get a pass. Harding had said to him, 'Here is your knife,' and

Sangret pocketed it. Linton Thorp at the trial suggested that Harding had returned the knife to someone other than Sangret. Harding would not be shaken.

It was never established exactly *how* Starratt knew this was Sangret's knife. Again, the force of *circumstantial* evidence comes into play as it does throughout the case. The knife was found near a wigwam that Joan and Sangret shared. It was perhaps a reasonable assumption, but it was an *assumption* nonetheless.

Sangret's version of events is of course different. The only mention of a knife in his first statement to Greeno is of his own Canadian issue, which he left with Joan at the wigwams and at the cricket pavilion. This was the tin-coloured one with the marlin spike she used to open cans with. In the second statement, having been specifically asked about knives, Sangret refers to the murder weapon. It was similar, he said, to an army issue knife, but had a black handle and Joan carried it in her handbag. She had been given it by her boyfriend, Francis, and she and Sangret had used it every day when they lived together. A military policemen (presumably Harding, although Sangret didn't know his name) showed Sangret the knife the day after he was released from the guardroom for having a girl on army property. Sangret told him it was Joan's knife. Sangret's version of events is that the knife was not returned to him and it was not returned to Joan. Although he had handled it many times, he was not certain that he could recognize it again. The unique hooked point appeared to have no significance for Sangret at all.

His testimony at the trial was rather different. Shown Exhibit 4 by Linton Thorp, Sangret denied that Joan had a knife like that. She used what was in effect his knife, with a single blade, a can-opener and a spike. The first time he had seen this particular black-handled pattern was in the Guildford police court. Many men he knew carried similar knives, even in the Canadian Army. Further confusion followed when Eric Neve mixed up Harding with Corporal Robert Talbot and asked if Talbot had returned the black-handled knife to Sangret. Sangret said he had not, that he had returned a

Canadian issue knife, Exhibit 34, to him. Mr Justice Macnaghten, alert as ever, corrected the name error.

There can be little doubt that Sangret was now lying to distance himself from that hook-bladed knife. It was obvious, from the forensic evidence he had heard, that the holes in Joan's skull and arm were made by that particular blade. So the black-handled knife that Francis had given to Joan became a Canadian issue one and Harding, rather than handing back no knife at all, now handed him back another Canadian issue knife. Are we looking, then at a murderer, covering his tracks very badly? Or a frightened, innocent man in the shadow of the noose?

The knife next surfaced on 27 November when Private Albert Brown of the Cape Breton Highlanders was clearing out the blocked drain of the shower in the guardroom. He put his hand up to the elbow in the narrow water outlet and pulled out paper and cigarette butts. The water still would not drain away so he plunged his arm down again and found more paper, cigarette ends, tinsel and Exhibit 4, the black-handled knife. He handed it to Lance-Corporal Albert Gero of his unit who had ordered him to clear the drain in the first place. The shower unit had been out of action since 0 October when Private Samuel King of the Royal Canadian Engineers had, as camp plumber, removed the fittings. The drain was not blocked then and he turned the water off so that the shower could not be used. He kept the mixer in his 'shop' for repairs. Gero handled the knife that Brown had found. He opened it and drew the blade across his hand to test its sharpness. He stuck the knife between the pipes and the wall and told Corporal Talbot to show it to Sergeant Wade when he came on duty.

Wade duly passed it to Sergeant Ballard of the Surrey police. Ballard was not asked about this at the trial, but Greeno had his murder weapon at last.

The prosecution argument, delivered by Eric Neve, was that Sangret stuffed the knife down the drain prior to his interview with Greeno, that is on 12 October. In fact, despite the bold assertions in his opening speech, Neve fell far short of *proving* anything of the sort.

> 'Corporal Stiles, who was in the guard room, remembers that during the time when the prisoner was in the guard room, he went to the wash-house which was adjoining ... and Stiles remembers that he went there either to have a wash or get a drink ... You will remember that I have drawn your attention to the fact that Corporal Stiles remembers the prisoner going, on that 12 October, into the wash-house.'

Greeno is even more adamant on this point.

> '[Sangret] went to the shower-room at the back to wash his hands but the water was cut off. He stayed three or four minutes and came out again.'

Theodore Stiles of the Military Police at Witley Camp effectively shot the ground from under Neve when, on the stand two days later, he denied remembering anything of the sort. 'Whilst you were there, did the accused at any time go to the wash-house?' 'I cannot remember.'

Neve would not give up. 'Can you remember whether at any time the accused went and had a drink or a wash?' 'I cannot remember. I did not have any conversation with him.'

The plank of the prosecution case had collapsed and it is an important one. It is all the more outrageous then that Greeno should stick to this story in *War on the Underworld* seventeen years later, as though it were a proven fact. We have already heard Private King's testimony that the shower drain was not blocked on 9 October when he came to dismantle the shower unit. It *was* blocked by 27 November. Does this mean that the knife *was* in the drain on 9 October and only the accumulation of cigarette ends and paper completed the blockage? Or did someone place the knife there *after* the 9th – indeed, after the 12th – knowing that the unit was out of action and that the knife was likely to be found when the unit was reassembled for use?

Keith Simpson puts an extraordinary gloss on the knife in the drain.

> 'Sangret really hanged himself when he hid the knife in the wash-house drain. He could only have known then of Joan's stabbing injuries if he had inflicted them himself. Why otherwise hide the knife? If he had kept the knife in his pocket and allowed Greeno to take it off him, the Crown would have had to rely solely on the medical evidence and I doubt if the jury would have convicted him.'

I cannot follow the logic of this paragraph, which concludes the Sangret chapter in Simpson's *Forty Years of Murder.* Assuming that Sangret killed Joan as charged, why not throw away the knife in Houndown Wood? Oddly, of course, a knife *was* found – and thrown away again – by a police officer conducting a search of the area. It *apparently* had no bearing and was like Exhibit 34 – the Canadian issue pattern – not Exhibit 4, the bone-handled murder weapon. But of course, we only have an inept policeman's word for that, a man anxious to play down the stupidity of his mistake. Why didn't Sangret, assuming the thought hadn't occurred to him in the heat of his killing, discard the knife on a route march or in Thursley or in Godalming or in Guildford or in Glasgow or anywhere else in fact where it would never be found? I don't believe that Sangret was remotely aware before his trial of the significance of the hook-pointed blade. Neither do I believe that he had the knife in his possession on 12 October, any more than he had on 14 September when somebody else killed Joan Wolfe.

Sangret was not a prisoner on 12 October. He could wander at will around the guard room and wash-house. But so, according to Corporal Talbot, could up to eighteen other people at any one time. Unless men were there as prisoners, they were not searched and even when they were, searches were not always carried out. The Military Police of course had the run of the place all the time. All that links August Sangret with the knife in the drain was that it was Joan's knife and he had been in the guardroom at the vaguely relevant time. No one saw him go into the wash-house at any time. Another piece of flimsy circumstantial evidence.

So if the forensic evidence of the weapons leaves us in fact with only the certainty that *someone* used them to kill Joan Wolfe, what of the chemical analysis carried out by Gerald Roche Lynch?

Eric Gardner was of the impression that Sangret's blanket, Exhibit 47 at the trial, had been washed. The inference was that this was done to remove bloodstains when he covered Joan's body in the dell at Houndown Wood. What was never established, because it was not asked, was why she or he was carrying the blanket when they had a perfectly good hiding place for it in the bushes behind the cricket pavilion over half a mile away. And which blanket was this? Sangret admitted to having at least three, one of which he found in Joseph Wells' presence behind the pavilion on the evening of Monday, 14 September. While the pair lived in their wigwams, they had two grey blankets and a greyish blue one. Two of these were issued to Sangret at Witley; the third was given to him at Fleet. None of them, according to Sangret, had been washed. These blankets were taken to the guardroom by the Provost's men towards the end of August, and when they were living in the cricket pavilion, they had one blanket only, one of the grey ones. If this is true, then how could Sangret have stashed the blanket behind the cricket pavilion with Private Wells, according to Greeno's theory, it was wrapped around the body of Joan Wolfe in Houndown Wood?

Roche Lynch had examined a water-bottle, a pair of battledress trousers and a blanket, respectively Exhibits 20, 40 and 47, on or shortly after 15 October when DS Hodge from the Yard delivered them to him. He could learn nothing from the water-bottle, but both the trousers and blankets gave him the impression of being washed. His initial remarks to Geoffrey Lawrence for the Crown were a classic piece of 'expert' fence-sitting:

> 'I tested the articles for the presence of blood ... [they] gave positive results suggesting the presence of blood, but in no case has it been possible to confirm the presence of blood or to establish whether the blood is human.'

He had used, as we have seen, the benzidine test which was inconclusive because it gave a positive reaction to things other than blood. His second test, the luminescence test, was a new one in 1942, but the weakness of this too was that it gave the same positive readings for non-serum substances. The fact that both tests gave a positive reading allowed him to say that he was 'strongly suspicious' that blood was present, though he admitted he couldn't be sure. Linton Thorp pressed Roche Lynch on this. Oxidizing agents like potassium nitrate and potassium iodine also give a positive result under the benzidine test. It would be a false positive, but there was no way of distinguishing it from real blood. In the case of the luminescence test, various salts of iron and various salts of copper also give false positives. In other words, neither test was conclusive to prove the presence of blood. Linton Thorp probably did not know that potassium nitrate and potassium iodine are by no means as exotic and unusual in a woodland glade or a cricket pavilion as the jury might think. Both are present in cauliflower, beetroot, tomatoes, radish, soya beans, dark fish-meat, melon and banana. Even allowing for the scarcity of melon and banana in wartime, we know that Joan bought tins of soup and jars of paste from the local shop. We know that she used her knife or Sangret's to open the tins. What more natural then that some of their contents should splash on to the blanket?

Roche Lynch confessed that he had insufficient data on which to work. The stains on the blanket did not possess enough blood – if blood it was – to be certain. The same problem applied to Sangret's trousers. In his second statement to Greeno, Sangret said he had two sets of battledress, the short combat jacket, trousers and webbing worn by most units in the Second World War. His Number Two battledress trousers he exchanged with Private Jesso, a bunk-mate, for a pair of his. He then exchanged these for a new pair at the Quartermaster's stores at the Educational Centre. He had an 'English tunic' and so the new pair of English trousers were designed to match it. Dyeing khaki was often a rather imprecise science, the Canadian shade being greener than the British. Roche Lynch admitted that he could not prove the existence of blood on Sangret's trousers and effectively demolished the prosecution's assertion that washing had removed all traces of blood by saying that it is 'almost impossible to wash the last traces of blood out of garments of this kind' because of the thickness of the serge fibres.

Having established without much room for doubt that the black-handled, parrot-beaked knife *was* the murder weapon, Roche Lynch failed utterly to find any blood on it. Justice Macnaghten fairly made the point that the Crown was not claiming there was blood on it, but why then did Roche Lynch cut the knife's cross-hatched handle and search the grooves for the stuff? The whole piece of analysis, bearing in mind Simpson's and Gardener's excellent work on the skull and arm wounds, seemed totally redundant and only pointed at Sangret if it also accepted that he wielded the knife in that murderous dell in Houndown Wood.

So, the forensic evidence against Sangret was inconclusive. That a birch stake had demolished Joan Wolfe's skull was clearly established. That she had previously been attacked with a knife believed to be Joan's and by some to have been carried by Sangret was likewise not in dispute. What none of this established was: who used these weapons on the dead girl?

What had Chief Inspector Edward Greeno got on Sangret? The prosecution had failed to prove that he slipped into the wash-house at the guardroom and dropped the deadly knife down the drain on 12 October, the day the Yard man took away Sangret's battledress, socks and boots – which again did not prove Sangret's part in murder. So far, Sangret 2, Scotland Yard 0.

At some point during his interrogations, conducted by Greeno with calm, fairness and honesty at all times, Sangret said, 'I guess you have found her. Everything points to me. I guess I shall get the blame.'

Greeno answered, 'Yes, she is dead,' and he cautioned him.

Sangret said, 'She might have killed herself.'

The prosecution implied, via the Chief Inspector, that this was an extraordinary statement to make unless he knew precisely how Joan had died and was trying to cover his tracks. Greeno had merely asked him to outline his relationship with Joan Wolfe. He had not told him she was dead. He hadn't even told him the girl was missing. But Sangret already knew she was missing. He had spent days looking for her, in all the old familiar places. And if a senior policeman comes to see you with a detective sergeant and a knot of uniformed men and gets permission to take you to a civilian police station and shows you items of clothing that belong to a girl you know and love, what are you supposed to think? That Joan Wolfe had lost her library ticket?

In connection with Greeno's first meeting with Sangret on 12 October, the Chief Inspector quoted Corporal Stiles, who had waited with Sangret until Greeno was ready to talk to him and who had said that he seemed agitated, pacing up and down and asking, 'How long does this go on? How long are they going to keep me here?' By the time Greeno did talk to Sangret, however, at eleven thirty, the man was calm and unruffled by the presence of a 'battleship' from Scotland Yard. We have already seen that Corporal stiles' version of events, on oath in a court of law, differed from his earlier version to the police. How seriously therefore can we take his account of Sangret's supposed attack of the jitters somehow implying guilt.

Greeno also ducked one vital question put to him by the judge.

'Was it your impression,' Macnaghten asked, 'that he did not know the body had been found?'

Greeno ignored impressions and merely said, 'I did not tell him anything about that.'

It became clear during cross-examination that much of Sangret's long statement was made in response to individual questions, especially the minute detailed description of clothes and possessions. Asked if he had heard anyone threaten Joan, Sangret replied, 'I have never said to her I will kill her.' Greeno no doubt found this damning, and the jury was supposed to too. I believe that what we have here is an innocent man defending himself against what he guessed would be the next line of inquiry. A guilty man would have said, 'Yes,' and concocted a fictitious person.

What are we to do with Sangret's curious suggestion that Joan might have killed herself? It either points to an imbecilic stupidity or to his innocence. Had Sangret shattered the girl's skull with the birch stake, he couldn't have imagined that Greeno would accept this as a viable method of suicide. Instead, it points to the fact that he had no idea precisely how the girl had died, and that he remembered her moodier moments in the pavilion. Early in September, perhaps three or four days before she died, Sangret remembered that Joan had got up in the middle of the night 'to make water'. She was gone for quite a time and when she came back she said, 'Do you know what I have been doing out there? I have been praying to God. I was asking God, I would like to die.'

Joan was crying and Sangret soothed her with the words, 'That is not a nice thing to wish for.'

Joan had sobbed, 'I don't like this suffering. I have no place to live.' She cried for four or five minutes and it was not helped by the fact that Sangret knew he'd be posted soon. The Canadians had landed in France. It was only a matter of time before the Reinforcement Units were sent in. 'I have lost one boy,' Joan said. 'He has gone back to Canada. I don't want to lose you.'

'If they want me to go, I've got to go,' he said.

'I will not let you go,' she told him.

And by an ironic twist of fate, Joan Wolfe never did let August Sangret go. Not to France, anyway.

We only of course have Sangret's word that this conversation ever took place. No one else speaks of Joan's unhappiness, but no one else knew her like he did and the only other person who might have done – her mother – was so consumed with bitterness about Joan that the once loving side of their relationship does not come through.

In all Sangret's long statements to the police, there is only one piece of damning evidence against him. I shall come back to it later.

In the meantime, let us do what British law is supposed to do and make the presumption that the accused is innocent. As has often happened, before and since, the police take the easiest line of approach. It is a commonplace that most murderers know their victims and this is particularly true of domestic situations. Joan was to all intents and purposes Sangret's wife – indeed she referred to him as her husband. In a case like this, Sangret would have been the prime suspect. I have no evidence that, for all Greeno and Webb interviewed scores of people, they ever looked seriously at anyone else. That was a mistake.

Joan was an obvious target. Today, such a runaway would be lured to the bright lights of a large city, not the perimeter fences of an army camp. But as we have seen, the war brought its own peculiarities. The Surrey police maintained that Joan was not a prostitute, but she *was* loose. As Macdonald Critchley wrote, '. . . her favours were easily secured.' We know that she had intercourse with Sangret in a public park after knowing him for only an hour or two – and this only two or three days after her earlier 'husband' had left her. We know that at least five other men featured in her life – and there may be others we do not know about.

The first was Francis Hearn. He was a Canadian soldier, seen by Kate Hayter in the company of Joan Wolfe at some time in July. Joan had told the old lady that she and Francis had married in London and that she was heartbroken at his being posted back to Canada. We have seen that Miss Hayter's testimony at the trial was woefully inadequate, claiming that Sangret had come to her house with Joan two days before they actually met. According to Sangret, and I can't think of a reason for him to lie, he *never* appeared at Kate Hayter's house with Joan. The old lady remembered that Joan used to walk regularly past her house on Kettlebury Hill with 'her husband whom I knew as "Francis" and "Pop".' A first reading of this trial testimony might imply that Francis and Pop were one and the same person, but a letter from Joan makes it clear that this was not so. Joan told Sangret that Hearn was her boyfriend but they could not get permission to marry because of his imminent posting. It is true that the girl wore a wedding ring, but whether she was ever legally or technically 'Mrs Hearn' is doubtful. Was the marriage story just one to impress other young, impressionable camp followers or fat girls like the one from Thursley who wandered the lanes with her for a while? Was the story intended to persuade Miss Hayter to allow the couple to stay at her house (although there is no evidence that they actually did)? And did she tell Sangret the truth so that she might replace the absent Francis with him?

Joan had spent a loveless childhood, abandoned by a father who had committed suicide and whose photo she carried, and effectively by a mother who had lost all patience with her. What she desperately needed was love and acceptance, from somebody, anybody. Perhaps if Joan told the marriage story often enough, it might one day come true. Certainly there was no mention of an inconvenient marriage ten days after Joan met Sangret when she was again discussing marriage, this time to him. Whatever the situation with Francis Hearn, whom Sangret believed had given Joan the hook-pointed knife used in her murder, we know that he had no hand in her death. The Provost-Marshal's Department checked – Francis had been shipped back home on 15 July; why is not recorded. Joan met Sangret two days later.

The second man hardly rated a mention in the story, but he was clearly interested in Joan. This was Private Hartnell, who shared Hut E2. Sangret refers to him as 'Hart' and on one occasion, he wrote a letter to Joan on Sangret's behalf. On 21 July, the second time that Joan and Sangret met, Hartnell was with him outside the Godalming fish and chip shop. Joan had just come out of the pictures and apparently already had a date with Hartnell. During the conversation that followed, Hart passed a note to Joan. She said, 'No.' He suggested that he and Sangret toss a coin to see who Joan would go with. Joan said she wouldn't have it that way. When Constable Halloran arrived, Hart wandered away.

Hartnell was not called to the trial. Was this his only contact with Joan Wolfe? It is anybody's away.

The third man in Joan's life is the shadowy figure of 'Pop'. Both Sangret and Kate Hayter mention him but only the old lady appears to have seen him. He was clearly a soldier and a (perhaps older) friend of Hearn's. In one of her letters which survived, Joan wrote to him in August 1942. The letter is headed 'Miss Joan Wolfe, c/o GPO, Godalming, Surrey, England.' 'My Dear Pop, I hope by this time that you have received my other letters. I shall be glad to hear from you. It seems ages since you have gone back [to Canada?]. I miss you *more than I do Francis* [my italics].'

Here was another man to whom Joan had given her heart – and perhaps her body too. He was probably the Private LaChance referred to briefly by the Provost-Marshal's office, who, like Hearn, had been posted back home on 15 July.

The fourth man in her life appeared as a prosecution witness at the trial. He was Rudolph Dworsky, a private in the Edmonton Regiment of the Canadian Army, who by virtue of his being born in the Sudetenland could claim to be both German and Czech. Czechoslovakia was only twenty-four years old at the time of the Sangret trial. It had been created out of the new jigsaw of Europe which emanated from the Versailles Treaty of 1919. In 1938, the area called the Sudetenland had been invaded by Hitler under his highly dubious policy of *Lebensraum*, whereby any territory containing German-speaking peoples was considered a legitimate part of the Third Reich. How Dworsky got out of the occupied territory and across to Canada is unknown but he met Joan in August when he was stationed at Camp 101, Witley. She was sitting by the roadside at the entrance to Jasper Camp, knitting. He had talked to her for about an hour when Sangret arrived.

'You find yourself a boyfriend?' the Métis had asked.

'No, don't mind me,' Dworsky said and wandered away. He saw the pair later as he sat opposite the Half Moon at Thursley. Two or three days later he saw Joan again, sitting by a tree stump near the road. She had Sangret's water-bottle and a Canadian issue army knife with her, in her handbag. How Dworsky could see into her handbag and why he should specifically refer to the knife was never explained. He spoke to her for a while, then Sangret appeared again. Dworsky walked away and sat reading a paper in the bushes on the common. He saw Joan again some days later while on a 'hardening course' and was unable to talk to her then.

Cross-examination by Linton Thorp elicited the fact that Dworsky's relationship with the dead girl was rather less casual than he made out. Sangret's statement said that Joan had told Dworsky that she was born in Germany (her mother did not mention this and various contacts I have made who knew the family doubt it too). Certainly the name Wolfe intrigued Dworsky.

'There is a German name very similar to that, is there not?' Linton Thorp asked.

'Yes,' said Dworsky. 'It is spelt W-o-l-l-f.'

Dworsky had asked the girl if she was German, but he could not, at the trial, remember the finer points of the conversation that Sangret clearly could from what Joan had told him. Dworsky may have felt a kindred spirit with the girl and doubly so when he saw her rosary and realized that they were both Catholic. They talked at that first hour-long meeting before Sangret arrived, about Joan's going back to Germany one day. This comes from Sangret's statement and Dworsky denied that it was true. Why? Was Sangret lying in order to implicate Dworsky in some way? He and Joan seemed to regard the Sudetenlander as a potential fifth columnist. After all, Germans and Italians living in Britain were interned just for *being* German or Italian. Here was a 'German' wearing the uniform of an ally. It didn't make a great deal of sense to an impressionable young girl and a less-than-sophisticated man from the Great Plains. Sangret's statement says that Dworsky was writing a book. An odd thing for the Canadian to make up unless it was true. He also says that Dworsky asked Joan to take off the wedding ring she was wearing and to meet him next day at five o'clock for a walk. Dworsky, curiously, could not remember asking Joan to remove a ring at all.

Was Dworsky lying in order to distance himself from Joan? He seemed at pains to avoid Sangret as far as possible, by walking away whenever he turned up. He explained at the trial that he liked Joan because she was the first civilian to speak to him in Britain and he wanted to renew their acquaintanceship: 'I do not know that there has to be a why to meet somebody and talk with them.' Joan gave him her Tunbridge Wells address and promised to write to him. Five o'clock came and went on the next day by Joan was not there.

He saw her later and she explained that she had gone to town (Godalming) instead, as though that said it all. Dworsky denied that he intended Joan to go out with him regularly, but for a man who simply wanted a little company, and who knew of Sangret's existence and his relationship with Joan, he seems to have been very persistent.

Private Raymond Deadman was no more honest that Dworsky in his reason for seeking Joan's company. He was in the process of transferring from the Canadian Army into the

133rd Infantry Regiment of the United States Army early in September and was based at Thursley Camp. With that extraordinary eye for detail that Sangret had, he remembered Deadman talking to Joan at the cricket pavilion. It was a Saturday between 1.30 and 2 p.m. Deadman was about twenty-one, according to Joan, and Sangret remembered him as 6 feet tall with a fair complexion, light brown hair, blue eyes, a round face, medium eyebrows, heavy build. He was clean shaven and wore khaki. The red flash on both arms was marked with white letters which Sangret thought read 'US'. Joan introduced him and Sangret said, 'Don't you like the Canadian Army?' Deadman's reply was a laconic, 'No.'

Deadman had been out for a walk, had seen the girl in 'a shack in one corner of the bowling green' (cricket pitch), and had spoken to her for some time. Although Joan told Sangret she had not seen the man before, it is clear from Deadman's trial testimony that the visit during which he met Sangret was his second that day. Joan introduced him as 'her husband', as she had earlier referred to Francis Hearn. Sangret seemed 'neutral' at this first meeting, but he quizzed Joan about Deadman when he'd gone. She'd told him she was going on Sunday to look for rooms in Elstead, to the north of Hankley Common, and Deadman had asked if he could go along. Sangret told Joan that *he* would go with her and that she was to wait for him.

In the event, Joan didn't. When Sangret arrived at ten on that Sunday morning, she had already gone. He waited for an hour and a half and the girl and Deadman appeared, having been for a walk over the common. According to Deadman, Sangret intercepted them before they reached the pavilion. He was angry and asked her why she hadn't done as he'd told her and waited for him. She replied that she'd got tired of waiting around. Sangret appeared 'very agitated'. Joan seemed afraid of him. Deadman changed the subject by saying that he was due to be posted on the next day to Northern Ireland. Then he left. Sangret and Joan ate later and he asked her is the American had 'tried to have connexions with her'. She said he did, but she wouldn't let him.

Linton Thorp effectively exposed Deadman for a hypocrite. The GI's story is that he took Joan on a two-hour walk across the common – passing very near, incidentally, to the spot where she was to die a week later – in order to find out if she was a 'decent sort of girl'. If he decided she was, he intended to help her. One wonders exactly how Deadman intended to do this with one or two days to go before he was posted overseas. If not, he would leave her along. He denied having intercourse with her; he denied kissing her; but the acid test of gauging her 'decency' apparently was to ask her to do both: 'I was close to the girl; we were sitting down. I broached the subject but she was unwilling so we left it at that.' It is hardly surprising that Sangret was annoyed when he found them together later.

Mr Justice Macnaghten seems to have bought Deadman's rather weak motivation entirely, if only for the obvious reason that the GI was posted elsewhere a week before Joan died – and an American base in Northern Ireland must make a pretty effective alibi.

Francis Hearn, Hartnell, 'Pop' LaChance, Rudolph Dworsky, Raymond Deadman – five men who are at least likely to have had some sort of sexual adventure, however brief, with Joan Wolfe during the summer of '42. This does not include men who we know knew her – men like William Featherby, the ARP warden who saw Joan living in the pavilion, or Arthur Robinson who watched her combing her hair, or the Military Police who watched the pair through their field telescopes and broke up their wigwams. Or any of the 100,000 troops living in the area that summer.

Of the non-locals, only Dworsky can be said to have been in the area when Joan died. No one, it is true, saw the Sudetenlander and Joan together at the times stated by Sangret, but then, no one was asked that particular question, either by the police or at the trial. In the minds of the Surrey constabulary, *Sangret* was the name associated with Joan. Why look any further? Greeno wrote years later, with the same assurance with which he disregards the truth about the wash-house incident, that Dworsky was 'also in the clear'. How this is so, he doesn't bother to tell us. It is a fact, however, that in terms of those men with the *opportunity* to murder, the police didn't even scratch the surface.

We have discussed means. We have discussed opportunity. What of motive? In his *Mammoth Book of True Crime*, the criminologist Colin Wilson includes the Wigwam Murder in a chapter called 'Unwanted Lovers' and he cites it as 'perhaps the last of the classic cases'. Wilson contends that no one else had a motive for killing Joan. My gloss on this would be that no one ever *established* a motive for anyone else killing Joan, which is not at all the same thing.

Wilson continues:

> 'In certain basic respects, the wigwam Murder is typical of its kind. Sangret was willing to sleep with the bedraggled 'wigwam girl' with the reputation for promiscuity, but not to marry her. Most men have a strong and automatic preference for 'virtue'; they may enjoy sleeping with promiscuous girls, but they prefer to marry virgins. Our permissive society has seen the gradual erosion of this idea; but in the Victorian age no one questioned it. The very fact that a girl *had* 'yielded her virtue' to a man was enough to make him feel a certain basic contempt for her and society was inclined to agree with him.'

He goes on to discuss a genuinely Victorian case where the concept fits. Unfortunately, it does not fit the Wigwam Murder itself. Wilson's contention is that Joan was a nuisance, perhaps even an embarrassment, and Sangret's solution was to kill her. The obvious question to ask next is: why?

Bruce Sanders in *Murder in Lonely Places* goes further. In a particularly unconvincing chapter called 'They Took to the Heather', Sanders attempts to recreate the lovers' last moments together:

> 'But he was suddenly without doubt about the kind of arrangement he had to make. The decision was becoming clearer in his furtive mind. It wasn't really a decision at all. It was something he had to do because *there was no alternative.*' [my italics]

The point, of course, which Wilson and Sanders have overlooked, is that there was a perfect alternative. The man who had probably made Joan pregnant, Francis, had taken it already. He had been transferred. There is nothing to suggest that this man, who was on the point of marrying the luckless Joan, ever tried to contact her again. Sangret had only to wait and the same option would have fallen to him. No one assumed that Witley Camp was the final destination for a Canadian soldier at war with Nazi Germany. Indeed, Sangret already been transferred – to Aldershot – by the time Greeno's inquiries were nearing fruition. In the constantly nomadic existence of soldiers in wartime, nothing lasted for ever.

And what if Joan had made a fuss, claiming that Sangret was the father of her unborn child, and had gone to his superiors? Although sergeant Wade was concerned about her and Major Gray had provided the necessary forms for marriage application, it was fairly apparent that Joan *was* a nuisance, to the Canadian Army and the local police. By 1942, largely as a result of two world wars, a vast social upheaval had taken place. Wilson's assertion that the last light of Victorian values still flickered in Sangret's alien mind simply does not work. The Canadian Army would have give Joan very short shrift indeed. And despite Sander's contention that Sangret felt trapped into an unwanted marriage by Joan, it is highly unlikely that he did. All he had to do was walk away.

Joan's pregnancy needs discussion too. Sangret seems to have accepted that the baby was his, but this is impossible given the dates involved. He first had intercourse with Joan on 17 July, two days after Francis Hearn left. Nine days later, Joan refers to the baby in a letter written from hospital where she had been taken after fainting: 'I am pretty sure we are going to have a tiny wee one ... We were taught that a baby before you are married is a sin ...' Fainting itself is not a symptom of pregnancy and it would be extremely rare for *any* symptoms to be apparent after so few days. Given Joan's peculiar lifestyle – living on borrowed food in the open air – the fainting and the fact that she had missed a period ('had not come on', in Sangret's phrase) are hardly surprising.

The scientists in the case were not able to prove a pregnancy at all. Keith Simpson was asked, 'Are you able to tell me whether she was pregnant or not?'

'No. The sexual organs had been so riddled with vermin infestation as to make it unjustifiable to form an opinion ... There may have been a pregnancy, with generation of gases after death dissolving it, and there may not have been a pregnancy at all.'

Dr Eric Gardner concurred. No report from the Warren Road Hospital exists on this point. It is unlikely that a laboratory pregnancy test would have been carried out in Joan's case, as the method in use at the time was both cumbersome and inaccurate, being used mainly in cases where a pregnancy would endanger the life of the mother. Even had such a test have been carried out, it would not have given a result before about the sixth week of pregnancy. Nor could internal examination for the confirmation of pregnancy give a result after the few days involved in this case. And no doubt, the young, insecure runaway, so desperate for her 'little Grey home in the West' that she drew on the wallboards of Thursley cricket pavilion, used the pregnancy to trap any man she could. For Joan, with her stultifying Catholic upbringing in a convent school, Wilson's suggestion of Victorianism is no doubt a probability – 'We were taught that a baby before you are married is a sin.'

All discussion of a motive, of course, overlooks one thing. The ferocity of the attack on Joan Wolfe indicates a sudden eruption of fury, not cold, careful premeditation or 'malice aforethought' in legal jargon. An attack with a knife to the *head* is not likely to kill, although Greeno wrongly thought it would – hence the use of the birch stake too. Joan was still up and running after the knife wounds. It was the stake that stopped her. In countries like France the recognition of the *crime passionnel* would have been enough to lessen the sentence. The more stolid English have never accepted mitigation in this way. As Eric Neve reminded the jury at the start of Sangret's trial, 'It is as much murder if you strike somebody across the head with a log of wood, or stab them, by which they come to their death, if that is done on the spur of the moment, as if you administer poison to them upon a plan which might have taken weeks or months or years to perfect.'

So, of the three basics in a murder case – means, opportunity and motive – only opportunity stands clear against Sangret. The means were available to anyone if we accept his version of events; the motive is particularly weak. Despite a general agreement that Sangret was surly, even sullen, there is no mention of a short fuse or uncontrollable temper. On the contrary – 'It takes a lot to upset an Indian chap.' Can we really believe that *no one* sharing Hut E2 with Sangret, or among the military policemen who moved him on and arrested him, or the civilian policemen who did likewise, would have seen any signs of the vicious temper necessary to crush the skull of another human being?

What of the unexplained elements in this case? Firstly, why did Sangret put up such a sustained pretence of trying to find Joan if he knew that she was lying dead, covered in a blanket and leaves in Houndown Wood? If Sangret was guilty, his pretence was quite extraordinary. Not only did he visit Kate Hayter's (twice) but he revisited the cricket pavilion several times, wandered to Godalming, even caught the bus to

Guildford in an effort to find her. Those who spoke of his indifference to her fate – Greeno and Wade at the time, various commentators since – have seen this as a symptom of guilt. It could also be a symptom of a man who did indeed feel he had had a narrow escape, that his passion *was* cooling after a few weeks with the girl. Equally it could be the macho reaction of a man of few words, embarrassed by the fact that his affair had been so public and that the girl had apparently left him. So, to different people he told different stories. She had gone 'on a scheme'. He had sent her home because she had no clothes coupons. She was living in the woods somewhere with his knife and his water-bottle. I think there was a change in Sangret's reaction to Joan's disappearance which will be discussed later. By all accounts, Sangret was no more than an averagely intelligent man. It takes quite a degree of intelligence to keep a lie alive in the positive way that Sangret did.

And again, Greeno is quick to defend the watertightness, as he saw it, of his case. Before the murder, Sangret barely mentioned the girl at all. After it, he was at pains to let everyone know that she was missing. This, again, is not strictly true. Sangret *had* discussed Joan and their marriage plans with Anderson and Bear from his own unit; with Hicks and Wade, the Provost's men; with Major Gray, his commanding officer; even with Superintendent Webb and the Godalming police. Rather a lot of people for Greeno to claim that 'Sangret had been a silent man'. And wouldn't a guilty man have hit upon a story to explain Joan's absence and stuck to it to all concerned? Or, if he couldn't think of one, simply shrug off nosy questions and say, 'I don't know where she is'?

Secondly, why hide the knife in the wash-house drain at the guardroom of Jasper Camp? A brighter man would have thrown it away in Houndown Wood or, better, anywhere else on the square miles of rough land that is Hankley, Thursley or Witley Common. Can we really believe that Sangret, with his limited grasp of concepts, was aware how forensically damaging that hook-bladed knife was? Contrary to Keith Simpson's assertions, he would have lost it – or kept it in his pocket. Only someone aware of the forensic importance of that point would have placed it where it was certain to have been found later.

Greeno's assertion is that Sangret hid the knife in the drain, unaware that the unit wasn't working, and here, of course, the Chief Superintendent has demolished his own argument. If Sangret had spent 'four of five minutes' in the washroom as Greeno claims, then he *must* have known the water supply wasn't in operation. Private King had dismantled the unity three days earlier and taken it away. Whoever put the knife down the drain was fully aware that the unit wasn't working, and that in the process of it being refitted, in all probability, the knife would be found.

Thirdly, why move Joan's body? Was she too exposed where she had fallen, in the dell at Houndown? Did he go back to make sure she was dead? Or did he want to hide the corpse more thoroughly? In which case, the last thing to do was to drag it up a fairly steep hill for nearly a quarter of a mile and cover it in loose earth in what was actually a very shallow grave on an exposed, almost treeless hilltop. Macdonald Critchley asks:

> 'Were these actions the product of mere stupidity; or an excess of cunning; or of superstition? Or was he, quite simply, crazy with drink at the time, and faltering in his judgement?'

The imputation about drink comes from nowhere. Admittedly, Sangret frequented pubs – he had first met Joan in one – but so presumably did thousands of other Canadian soldiers. We have here, once again, the unconscious racism: the old myth about the 'red man's' aversion to 'firewater'. It has no substance and stems from the fact that 'Indian whiskey' as supplied to the tribes on the plains in the nineteenth century was highly toxic stuff, composed as it was of 'one gallon of raw alcohol, three of water, a pound of tea, a pound of shredded black tobacco, a quarter of black molasses, a handful of red peppers and a scoop of ginger'. Small wonder it was called 'firewater'.

Critchley's 'excess of cunning' escapes me. It smacks of the same hindsight that Superintendent Tom Roberts used when he found Sangret's statement full of cunning and guile. It is always risky for a murderer to return to the scene of the crime in case he is spotted or leaves incriminating evidence. I really cannot understand his reasoning here.

The superstition angle is based on the fact that the Plains Indians habitually bury their dead on high ground. Was Sangret following a deep-rooted, almost subconscious compulsion to follow ancient tribal ways? A fascinating concept, but one not without its problems. There are no hills on the plains. On the contrary, the horizon is monotonously flat. The Indians bury their dead on platforms fixed on poles above ground level so that wolves and other animals could not eat them (this did not preclude the scavenging of vultures, of course). Mere burial on high ground is not therefore Plains Indian custom.

That leaves us with Critchley's 'mere stupidity'. Sangret's mental makeup would certainly make this a possibility, but what was in his mind at the time we can only surmise.

My surmise is that Sangret *did* find Joan Wolfe's body, where someone else left her in the dell at Houndown. What could he do then? Report his find to the Military Police? An illiterate Métis with a police record of violence? Perhaps he *was* trying to do what his ancestors had done, given the limitations of the situation in which he had found the girl. He gave her the best burial he could on the highest ground he could find where she wouldn't be found. Was it only the chance run of a tank rack that spoiled all that? Is that why his mood changed and with it his reaction to questions about Joan? From looking earnestly for her in all the old familiar places, he suddenly stopped and began shrugging when colleagues asked him where she had gone. Once he'd made the grim discovery and taken the conscious decision to bury Joan, he was then stuck with it. How would it have looked if he'd said, 'Yes, well, I *did* find her body, but I didn't tell anyone about it'?

In the second meeting with Greeno, Sangret said one thing to the Chief Inspector which damned him in the eyes of the police and the court. When Greeno took him to the dell in Houndown Wood where Joan had died, Sangret said, 'I do not want to go over there. I do not know that place.'

Greeno sensed that Sangret did know that place because that was where he had stabbed and bludgeoned Joan Wolfe to death. I believe he knew it because he had found there the rotting body of the girl whom, for all his rough ways and after his fashion, he had loved.

Sangret's testimony at the trial was that various witnesses were lying, but he could not offer a reason why. My contention is that his average intelligence and sullen alienation precluded this. The reason is that he was disliked, not because he was August Sangret, a not very pleasant man with s string of brushes with Canadian law, not because he broke regulations and slept with an English runaway, but because he was a Métis. He was an outsider. He was different. Sangret sadly mentions in his statement to Greeno some of the twenty-five men who shared Hut E2 with him. Corporal Thompson, Martin Ducherne, Anderson, Jesso and 'Mary'. None of them spoke for him at his trial. Not even his old friend from Battleford, 'Johnny' Wells, who actually spoke for the prosecution.

Let me pose the question slightly differently. If Sangret did not kill Joan Wolfe, who did? The answer is, perhaps, someone in the Provost-Marshal's department at Witley Camp. Sangret was unpopular. He was making a nuisance of himself bringing a girl on to army property. That girl had been in the guardroom herself. She was 'easy'; she was available. Had one of the MPs done what Dworsky and Deadman and Sangret himself had done? Made advances to Joan on that Monday morning, 14 September, when he knew Sangret would be at a class? Had they gone for a walk in Houndown Wood? We know that was her style. Had she, as Deadman maintained she had done to him, turned the man down? Had he snatched up Sangret's knife, which was either already in his pocket, or back in Joan's handbag, the handbag Dworsky had looked into? The handbag the murderer took away with him when it was all over? Had she screamed at him? Cursed him? Threatened to tell Sangret? Had he lost his temper, lashed out, stabbed her in the head (wounds that were likely to have been inflicted by a taller man than Sangret, if Joan, as was probable, was standing up at the time), then chased her, his blood up, with a birch stake in his hand? And had he then returned, as if from a routine patrol of the area, after roughly covering her battered body with autumn's early leaves?

Did he then have time to think? He'd killed Joan with a birch stake shaped and fashioned at both ends. He knew that because Sangret's wigwams were familiar to all the MPs it would be assumed that this was Sangret's handiwork. He'd stabbed Joan with her own knife, the one associated with Sangret. Joan had been Sangret's girl; the MPs knew that perfectly well – they'd watched them through their field glasses. Why not complete the circle and make sure that Sangret would 'take the rap'? The girl's body lay only partially covered, near the road. It was only a matter of time before she was found. He'd wait for a chance to plant the tell-tale knife, the knife whose hooked point had been noted by at least two MPs on the case. That chance came on 12 October when Greeno came to the guardroom to talk to Sangret. What better place to hide it, knowing it would not flush away, than the U-bend of the wash-house drain, where the already broken shower unit meant that extensive plumbing repairs would ensure that it would be found.

An implausible theory? I don't think so. No more implausible certainly than the one the prosecution produced. And talking of implausible, Greeno, in *War on the Underworld*, posits the theory that Sangret used the excuse of blackberrying on 15 September to nip back to Houndown Wood to rebury the corpse of the girl he had killed the day before. *A burial in broad daylight between a road and a Marine camp near the place where the tanks train.* For the sake of his career, it was probably just as well that Greeno didn't come out with this nonsense in court. What we have in this case is a motiveless murder, carried out by a man whose profile was dangerously high. Sangret was what his fellow Canadians would have called a 'fall guy', a 'patsy'.

Greeno said later that Sangret confessed to the murder before he died. This is from an unattributed source. It is unlikely to have come from the Catholic chaplain who visited the man daily before his execution, for that would have broken the sanctity of the confessional. If it came from a prison officer, unsupported and unrecorded, it must be taken with a large pinch of salt. And anyway, it was very much in Greeno's interest for the confession to be genuine. How else can a policeman conducting a murder inquiry, which ends in a man's death, sleep again?

'He confessed,' Greeno said confidently seventeen years later, 'before he died and this is where I quarrel with the rules. It is never announced when a murderer confesses. But why not? There are always cranks and crackpots to argue that some wicked policeman has framed the poor fellow. So why make an official secret of the fact that the policeman did his job?'

'I didn't do it,' Sangret had said, 'Someone did, but I'll have to take the rap.' Did that ambiguous 'someone' mean that Sangret knew perfectly well who had done it? If he did, his knowledge died with him.

He took the rap, at Wandsworth on 14 April 1943, in the Moon of the Grey Goose. Public hangmen do not talk over much about their work. Albert Pierrepoint had been appointed to the grim post the previous year. He hanged Derek Bentley and Timothy Evans after the war and very possibly other innocent men. He also hanged a lot of guilty ones. There is a tendency to shoot the messenger in these cases. Pierrepoint died in 1993, in an old people's home, his mind gone, his fingers ever fiddling with knots. In the 1940s and 1950s, he was *the* practitioner *par excellence*, carrying out with awesome speed and efficiency the sentence prescribed by the courts: a ghastly job, but one performed 'on behalf of the state'.

There is no mention of August Sangret in his book, *Pierrepoint; Executioner*. Pierrepoint's war — or at least his memories of it – dealt with the infamous Nazi elite he hanged at Nuremberg. Small fry like Sangret had no place in that. And his sometime assistant, Syd Dernley, did not appear in post until 1949. My official request to the authorities for any information on Sangret's execution met with the now inevitable answer that a hundred-year embargo is placed on capital offences. In the year 2043, when I shall be ninety-three years old, no doubt I'll try again!

The likelihood is that the cool, efficient Pierrepoint hanged August Sangret in the execution shed at Wandsworth Prison seconds after nine o'clock in the morning. If all went according to plan, a knot of officials entered the condemned cell with Pierrepoint and his assistant Henry Critchell. Sangret would have had to have walked perhaps twelve or fifteen paces to the trap. His hands would have been pinioned behind him, his ankles strapped together. A white cap would have been placed over his head and face, the noose slipped around his neck. One final check that all was secure and Sangret would have stood alone on the edge of eternity. Pierrepoint would have pulled the lever and gravity would do the rest. Sangret's spine would have snapped at the third vertebra. He would have dangled there for an hour, to make sure that life was extinct.

It was minutes after that that Molly Lefebure saw him again, on the post-mortem table as Keith Simpson examined him officially to give the cause of death. 'He lay there,' she remembered, '… muscular, well built, almost good enough for one of Fennimore Cooper's novels, his handsome bronzed skin marked only by the imprint of the hangman's noose around his neck …'

Even after death, August Sangret exerted a certain animal magnetism. And she noticed, on his forearm, a tattoo of the name he never called the girl he loved – 'Pearl'.

The Sangret papers tell what is left of the story. The brief description of Sangret on the date of his discharge from the army – the date of his death – has his age wrong by two years. He was 5 feet 4½ inches tall, with dark complexion, brown eyes and black hair. Across the discharge certificate is stamped the single word 'Deceased'. The official cause of death, on a document dated 4 May, reads, 'Injury to brain and spinal cord consequent upon judicial hanging.' His remains were buried in the communal grave in Wandsworth Prison, unmarked, at half-past one on 29 April, while the other prisoners were having lunch. A copy of the death certificate and burial report were sent to Napoleon Sangret, his father.

Four days later, a Committee of Adjustment met at Laurentide Camp, Witley by order of Colonel M K Greene, the Commandant of the Second Canadian Reinforcement Unit. The Committee decided to send to Napoleon Sangret the personal effects of his dead son. They consisted of five assorted snapshots, the subjects of which are unknown, a black leather belt, a waist belt, a water-bottle, a jacket sweater and two shoulder straps. Total value £1 and a ha'penny. His uniforms were returned to the Unit Quartermaster.

For the rest of the '40s, correspondence winged its way between Ottawa and Battleford as the Sangrets argued over the allowance August was due, as they counted to an extent as his dependants. By January 1950 his family were sent his war medals – the Defence medal, the Canadian Volunteer Service medal and clasp and the War Medal. A handwritten note says, 'Do not issue memorial bar. Died – judicial hanging.'

Interestingly, Sangret was included, on 3 May 1943, in 'Overseas Canada's Roll of Honour'. All it says is 'Royal Canadian Service Corps – Sangret, August, Pte. L27572.'

My letter to the Sangrets of Battleford elicited no reply.

Neither Keith Simpson nor Molly Lefebure could understand why the jury in the Wigwam Murder case had recommended mercy. Were those twelve men and true unhappy with the appallingly unsatisfactory situation of circumstantial evidence? The duty of the prosecution in this – as in every – case, is to prove the accused guilty beyond a shadow of a doubt. There were many shadows circling round the case of the wigwam girl – as many shadows as lengthened on the summer evenings in Houndown Wood, when the sun died behind the trees. There were many doubts about the guilt of August Sangret. A better jury would have expressed them by finding him innocent, since, in the absence of proof, that is all, in conscience, they could have done. Instead, they succumbed to the blandishments of Eric Neve and Geoffrey Lawrence, to the tragedy of a hapless girl to whom the world was unkind. They were blinded by the dazzling certainties of Keith Simpson, Eric Gardner, Gerald Roche Lynch. And I doubt they were impressed by the dour, sullen August Sangret who was so very different from themselves. All they did in the end was to recommend mercy, hoping that someone else would save the man they had so unjustly condemned. It was not enough that there was a likelihood that Sangret killed the wigwam girl, even a probability. They had to be sure *beyond a reasonable doubt* and, despite the silence and sanctity of the jury room, I am prepared to bet that they were not.

Any number of men might have killed Joan Pearl Wolfe. But one thing is certain – there is no proof that August Sangret did. In a moment during the trial, Mr Justice Macnaghten had said, referring to the forensic traces on blanket, trousers and knife, '. . . there is no evidence that there was ever blood on this man.'

Perhaps the Lord had mercy on him after all.

Afterword

Since the writing of *The Wigwam Murder*, the world has turned, but nothing new has emerged in this particular case. The aftermath of *Let Him Have It, Chris* was astonishing. Not only was the murder conviction against Derek Bentley overturned, but the law that made it possible, that of joint felonious enterprise, has been repealed. The Bentley decision, the hanging of an educationally subnormal boy for a murder he did not commit, was controversial from Day One. The Wigwam case was not. There was a war on, newsprint itself was in scarce supply and the jury was sufficiently swayed by the evidence to find August Sangret guilty. Despite their recommendation to mercy, no mercy was extended to the outsider, the loner without any real friends. In the book you have just read, I find the evidence against Sangret circumstantial and the verdict unsafe, but I concede I may be in a minority of one.

Thames Television, as they then were, contacted me soon after publication. The story of an Indian living in a wigwam in rural Surrey intrigued them (though I suspect they may have had their wires crossed with Grey Owl, Archibald Belaney, 1888-1938) and I 're-enacted' the murder on location, swinging a birch branch towards the camera lens and scrabbling through the undergrowth. Since this was a local news 'feature', there was no fee and I am not even sure it was ever shown.

Very belatedly, I was contacted by a member of the Sangret family who expected payment because I had 'used' his forebear in a book. I decided not to reply to tell him that that was not how publishing worked!

Years later still, I was asked by the Historical Society at Scotland Yard to talk to them on the case. The evening was well attended; I showed my power-point presentation and I hope a good time was had by all. The famous 'Black Museum', which I have now visited twice, thanks to the Metropolitan Police's good offices, could not help with the Sangret case because it came under the jurisdiction of the Surrey police at the time.

The most bizarre follow-up to the *Wigwam Murder* was a letter out of the blue from a man who claimed to be August Sangret's son. He could not understand how I could have got my facts so wrong, because his mother had told him that Sangret was his father and he had not been born until 1950. Since this was some seven years after the Métis' execution, I could not understand that either.

Welcome to the world of true crime!

Bibliography

BAILEY, Guy [C.K. Simpson], *The Fatal Chance*, Peter Davies 1969
BLAND, James, *The Crime Diary*, Futura, 1987
BRUCE, Sealey D. and LUSSIER, Antoine S., *The Métis: Canada's Forgotten People*, Pemmican, 1975
BYRNE, Richard, *Prisons and Punishments of London*, Grafton, 1992
CRITCHLEY, Macdonald, *Notable British Trials Volume 83*, William Hodge & Co, 1959
GARDINER, Juliette, *'Over Here' – The GIs in Wartime Britain*, Collis and Browne, 1992
GAUTÉ, J.H.H. and ODELL, Robin, *The Murderer's Who's Who*, Pan, 1980
GAUTÉ, J.H.H. and ODELL, Robin, *Murder Whatdunnit*, Pan, 1982
GOODWILL, Jean and SLUMAN, Norma, *John Tootoosis*, Pemmican, 1984
GREENO, Edward, *War on the Underworld*, John Long 1960
JENNESS, Diamond, *Indians of Canada*, University of Toronto Press, 1967
LEFEBURE, Molly, *Murder on the Home Front* (Reprint of *Evidence for the Crown*, 1954) Grafton 1990
ROBERTS, Tom, *Friends and Villains*, Hodder and Stoughton, 1987
SANDERS, Bruce, *Murder in Lonely Places*, H. Jenkins, 1959
SIMPSON, Keith, *Forty Years of Murder*, Granada, 1980
St J. BARCLAY, Glen, *The Empire is Marching*, Weidenfeld, 1976

STACEY, Col. C.P., *Official History of the Canadian Army in the Second World War,* Vol 1.

STORY, Norah, *The Oxford Companion to Canadian History and Literature*, OUP, 1967

TANNER, Ogden, *The Canadians, The Old west*, Time Life 1977

TULLETT, Tom, *Murder Squad*, Granada, 1981

WILSON, Colin, *The Mammoth Book of True Crime*, Robinson Publishing 1988

A History of the Original Peoples of Northern Canada, McGill-Queen's University Press, 1974

The Native Americans: The Indigenous Peoples of North America, Salamander, 1991

The National Archives of Canada, Personnel Records Centre, National Defence Headquarters, Ottawa, Canada.